Brimming with creative inspiration, how-to projects, and useful information to enrich your everyday life, Quarto Knows is a favorite destination for those pursuing their interests and passions. Visit our site and dig deeper with our books into your area of interest: Quarto Creates, Quarto Cooks, Quarto Homes, Quarto Lives, Quarto Drives, Quarto Explores, Quarto Gifts, or Quarto Kids.

Inspiring | Educating | Creating | Entertaining

© 2017 Quarto Publishing Group USA Inc.

First published in 2017 by Voyageur Press, an imprint of The Quarto Group, 401 Second Avenue North, Suite 310, Minneapolis, MN 55401 USA. T (612) 344-8100 F (612) 344-8692 www.QuartoKnows.com

Voyageur Press titles are also available at discount for retail, wholesale, promotional, and bulk purchase. For details, contact the Special Sales Manager by email at specialsales@quarto.com or by mail at The Quarto Group, Attn: Special Sales Manager, 401 Second Avenue North, Suite 310, Minneapolis, MN 55401 USA.

10 9 8 7 6 5 4 3 2 1

ISBN: 978-0-7603-5274-8

Library of Congress Cataloging-in-Publication Data

Names: Peterson, Chris, 1961- author.
Title: The pallet book : DIY projects for the home, garden, and homestead /
  by Chris Peterson.
Description: Minneapolis, Minnesota : Voyageur Press, 2018. | Includes index.
Identifiers: LCCN 2017017746 | ISBN 9780760352748 (pb)
Subjects: LCSH: Woodwork--Patterns. | Pallets (Shipping, storage, etc.) |
  Wood waste--Recycling.
Classification: LCC TT180 .P464 2018 | DDC 684/.08--dc23
LC record available at https://lccn.loc.gov/2017017746

Acquiring Editor: Thom O'Hearn
Project Manager: Jordan Wiklund
Art Director: James Kegley
Cover Designer and layout: Simon Larkin
Project design: Chris Peterson
Builder/photographer: Chris Marshall

On the front cover: Pallets can be used to create attractive and useful projects around the home, including Adirondack chairs (top left), bookshelves and storage (top right), side tables (bottom right), and even provide opportunities for decoration such as wall clocks (bottom left) and more.
On the back cover: Pallet garden bench and planter.

Printed in China

The
Pallet Book

DIY Projects for the Home, Garden, and Homestead

CHRIS PETERSON

VOYAGEUR
PRESS

CONTENTS

WORKING WITH PALLETS

YARD & GARDEN PROJECTS

3 STORAGE

4 FURNISHINGS & DÉCÓR

INTRODUCTION

The book you have in your hands (or the e-reader you're reading it on) has spent part of its life on a pallet. So have the vast majority of small items in your home, from food to furniture to the various parts of your house itself. Pallets are the stage on which the great drama of commerce plays out. Okay, maybe that's a bit much. But they are the standardized platforms that make it easy to ship stuff.

And what a platform. Pallets are ingenious in their simplicity. They're sized so that professionals—from warehouse planners to shipping companies—can play what amounts to sophisticated games of Tetris to get the most out of a truck, railcar, shipping container, or any warehouse. Pallets are lightweight, but can support incredibly heavy loads. A pallet is so economical as to be disposable, but so durable that a single pallet can survive thousands of miles and ton upon ton of accumulated weight.

That usefulness is why pallets are everywhere. According to the US Forest Service, there are two billion pallets in use in the United States alone. The vast majority of those are wood (there are metal, plastic, composite, and recycled-material pallets as well). More than four hundred million new pallets will be produced in any given year to replace those that are damaged or destroyed—including the more than one hundred million that will simply be thrown out.

Those waste pallets are upcyclers' gold.

You may not think of yourself as an upcycler, but if you ever take the opportunity to reclaim a pallet and repurpose all or part of it into something new, that's just what you are. And why wouldn't you embrace that label? With all the discarded pallets lying around coast to coast, you'd almost be crazy not to turn them into something useful and interesting. Worried that your DIY skills aren't up to the task? Don't be. Working with pallets is amazingly simple

and requires only basic crafting abilities. If you can put together an IKEA bookshelf, you can turn a pallet into something useful and delightful. You also won't need a boatload of tools. Most of what can be done with a pallet requires about five basic tools that you probably already own.

Getting started is as easy as turning the page to Chapter 1: Working with Pallets. That riveting read will quickly teach you how to modify, remodel, or deconstruct a pallet with a minimum of fuss. This basic grounding in the anatomy of a pallet will set you up to tackle the projects in the chapters that follow. You'll find a whole range—from the incredibly easy and small (lovely tea light candleholders anyone?)

The easiest way to upcycle pallets is to sand them down, paint them, and stack them like the sofa in this living room. The projects in this book, however, go a bit further than that, using pallets to create structurally sound furnishings, storage, and more.

This rough-and-tumble compost bin and access ramp makes good use of the rugged nature of most pallets.

to complex but still doable large projects that will provide low-cost, handsome options for home furnishings (how about a pallet platform bed that you can construct in about half a Saturday?). The common denominator? Ease. These projects are easy to understand, with simple-to-follow steps that make the constructions a breeze to finish. Oh yeah, they're all stylish and fun too.

More than anything else, though, all these projects are rewarding. Whether you're building a **Wine and Liquor Bottle Rack** (page 79) or whipping up some **Pallet Plant Markers** (page 47), the cost will be close to zero. You'll have the satisfaction of making something that you would otherwise have had to buy, and even more satisfaction knowing that you probably saved the wood from going right into an already crowded landfill.

So if you know it's easy, environmentally beneficial, fun, productive, and rewarding to your soul and your pocketbook, there's really only one question left: What are you waiting for?

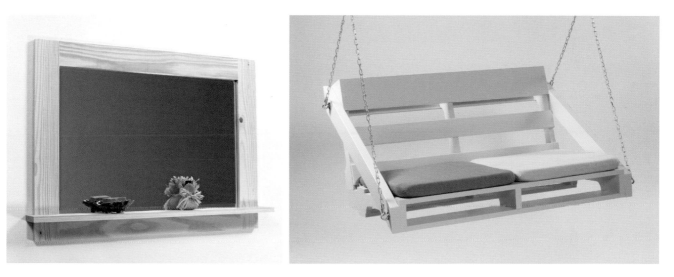

1 WORKING WITH PALLETS

One of the most amazing things about pallets is that for something that is so useful and adaptable, a pallet is actually an incredibly simple construction. That makes it easy to take apart or modify. However, even though they are all constructed in a similar fashion, there are many different kinds of pallets with many variables in how they're made. That variety reflects how different pallets are meant to be used with a forklift.

All pallets are designed to be picked up and moved by a forklift, the most efficient method for loading, unloading, and moving shipped goods.

THE ANATOMY OF THE PALLET

The basic difference among pallets is the way in which forklift blades slide under the pallet. A pallet can be designed as "two-way," accessible from only two opposite sides, or "four-way," accessible from any direction. Obviously, this affects how the pallet can be used. To complicate matters, there are partial four-way pallets with cutouts in the side stringers (the sturdier boards that support the deck boards and run perpendicular to them). These pallets are meant to be lifted or skidded from the front or back, or lifted from the sides.

Pallets are also designated either "stringer" or "block," depending on how they are constructed. Stringer pallets use two-by-fours or two-by-sixes on edge, as the three main supports for the top and bottom deck boards. Block pallets use corner four-by-four blocks, connected by stringer boards on top that serve as nailers for the top deck boards, and bottom boards running both ways.

Stringer Pallet

Block Pallet

Different manufacturers use different widths and thicknesses of deck boards. The most common are one-by-fours, or an actual size of three-quarters inch by three and a half inches. End or "lead" deck boards are often wider, such as one-by-sixes (actual size of three-quarters inch by five and a half inches). In reality, pallet construction is not overly precise. Manufacturers can use unsightly wood that wouldn't be marketable as boards. There is also a lot of variance in the different pieces. Although stringers are usually standard sizes, depending on where you find the pallet and who manufactured it, deck boards can range in thickness from three-eighths inch to three-quarters inch. That means that you may have to adapt the projects in this book to the thickness of deck board on the pallets you salvage.

COMMON US PALLET SIZES

SIZE	USE
48 × 40	General, grocery store
42 × 42	Paint, wire spools
48 × 48	Metal drums
48 × 42	Chemicals, beverage industry
40 × 40	Dairy products
48 × 20	General retail
36 × 36	Beverage
48 × 45	Automotive parts

COMMON INTERNATIONAL PALLET SIZES

SIZE	CONTINENT
39.37 × 47.24	Europe, Asia
44.88 × 44.88	Australia
43.30 × 43.30	Asia
31.50 × 47.24	Europe

OTHER PALLET TYPES

The pallet formats shown here are the most common. However, there are other formats. Most any wood pallet can be adapted for use in the projects in this book.

Two way

Two way, wing

Four way

Two way, reversible

Pallets are also available in a range of overall dimensions. The most common in the United States is forty-eight inches by forty inches, but different industries use different size pallets to ship material and equipment specific to a given industry. There are also smaller units meant to ship smaller loads or to be used in smaller delivery trucks or vehicles.

International pallets add even more sizes into the mix, not only because they're using metric measurements, but because European trucks and shipping containers are often sized to much different dimensions than American vehicles.

All these variables mean that you need to keep an open mind when reclaiming pallets. The units you find for reuse may well be far from "standard," but that doesn't make them less usable. The pallets specified in all the projects in this book are standard stringer pallets with nominal two-by-four stringers, and nominal one-by-four decking; we assume an overall width of forty-eight inches by forty inches. We have used "notched" stringer pallets (partial four-way) for many of these, because they are some of the most commonly available types of pallets. The notch can make for an interesting appearance, depending on where it falls in the span of the cut piece. However, the notches can also present design and structural challenges, depending on what you're building. Where there might be structural concerns—such as a weight-bearing leg—we've turned to "unnotched" two-way stringers.

That said, all these projects have been developed for maximum adaptability, to allow you to customize the plans to whatever pallets you may have reclaimed.

A standard "partial four-way" stringer pallet. Note the notches in the side stringer that allow for forklift blades but still provide a surface for a limited number of bottom deck boards.

Pallets of all kinds can be used to make furnishings and accents that are limited only by imagination. Here, block pallets have been chopped up and reassembled to make a chunky, rustic living room sofa and coffee table. It may not be the height of luxury, but they are durable, usable, and basically free!

Uniformly colored pallets like these should be avoided. The color is usually a sign that the pallet was used to ship a particular material, often chemicals or other potentially toxic substances.

THE HUNT FOR PALLETS

It's not hard to find pallets for reclamation because they're used to ship so many materials and products. The trick is to locate pallets that are in fairly decent shape and that aren't spoken for. Although the easiest places to find a wealth of pallets are behind big-box stores and large retailers where they may be stacked haphazardly, many of these companies have agreements with recyclers to bulk collect used pallets. (Remember, pallets in good shape can be reused again and again.)

Unless the pallets have obviously been discarded as trash—on the curb during large trash pickup day or in a local dump—you'll need to ask permission to take them. That said, many companies are more than willing to have you cart them off. That includes construction companies on large construction sites, where they often don't have anywhere to store pallets to keep them out of the path of workers and vehicles, and they may not have arranged to have the pallets removed. You may also get lucky and find whole dumpsters full of unbroken or slightly damaged pallets.

Regardless of where you find them, you'll want to make absolutely sure that the pallets you reclaim are safe for reuse. This involves determining if they have been used to transport any toxic or dangerous materials and avoiding those that have. Fortunately, most pallets are marked on the top, bottom, or sides, and the markings often tell the story of where the pallet came from and what it carried.

COMMON PALLET MARKINGS

IPPC [a]: This is the mark of the International Plant Protection Convention and certifies that the wood used in the pallet does not contain invasive plant or insect species. IPPC pallets must be treated to kill any organisms remaining the wood—either through debarking or heat treatment.

DB [b]: The pallet has been debarked, but is otherwise untreated. Generally safe for projects.

HT [b]: Heat treating pallets kills organisms that might have survived milling, rendering the pallet safe for use—especially in projects.

KD [b]: This means the wood was kiln dried. For the purposes of an upcycling project, it's the same as heat-treating. Kiln drying also ensures that the wood will be less likely to warp or deform when you reuse it.

MB [b]: The pallet has been treated with methyl bromide and should be avoided for upcycling.

EPAL: This is the European Pallet Association logo; it certifies that the pallet has been debarked and heat treated, and verifies that the wood is safe to use in projects.

EUR: This predates the current European Pallet Association designation and you cannot reliably be sure of which chemicals may have been used on the pallet. Many upcyclers avoid pallets with this mark.

PRL: This stamp proves verification by the Packaging Research Laboratory, indicating that the pallet has been treated with high-temperature heat treatment and does not contain toxic chemicals. This is a good sign for anyone looking to upcycle the pallet.

Colored pallets: Pallets that are uniformly colored all over with red, blue, or brown are used by specific industries such as pool and spa manufacturers. These have likely been exposed to toxic chemicals and are subsequently not used for upcycling.

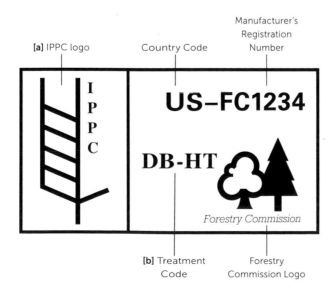

[a] IPPC logo   Country Code   Manufacturer's Registration Number

US–FC1234

DB-HT

Forestry Commission

[b] Treatment Code   Forestry Commission Logo

DECONSTRUCTING PALLETS

Once you've laid your hands on some safe and structurally sound pallets, you'll probably need to modify them for whatever purpose you have in mind. Although several of the projects in this book make use of whole pallets, you'll often need to deconstruct a pallet to one degree or another for upcycling.

When it comes to taking pallets apart, the right tools will save you time, money, and effort, and can even prevent injury. The job is not necessarily as easy as it might appear, because pallet manufacturers use very stubborn fasteners, such as shank nails, and trying to separate the pieces can lead to the destruction of much usable wood. Often, the best way to remove deck boards from stringers or blocks is to actually cut the nails. Occasionally you'll be faced with sacrificing a section of wood that simply can't be separated from another section. In any case, here's a list of basic deconstruction tools that are also used to craft many of the projects in the book.

Hammer. A basic claw hammer is the crudest and least effective method to separate pallet boards. Even using a wedge to help pry a board up, the hammer will often destroy the end of a board rather than budge the fasteners.

Pry bar. A good pry bar can give you just the right amount of leverage exactly where you need it to loosen stubborn boards, but using a pry bar to take apart a pallet requires patience and a great deal of effort. It can also lead to breakage and, specifically, end splitting.

Pallet buster. Pallet busters are specially constructed to exert maximum force on the fasteners without cracking boards. The long handle and shaped tines use physics to require a minimum of effort for a maximum of force. The downside is that these tools tend to be pricey. Consequently, it only makes sense to purchase one if you plan on breaking down quite a few pallets.

Reciprocating saw. Known commonly by the brand name Sawzall, this hardworking saw can tear through stringers, blocks, and boards alike, as if they were butter. Equipped with a metal-cutting blade, the saw can cut between boards and stringers, severing stubborn fasteners. When the board can't be removed, or a thick stringer needs to be cut to size, a reciprocating saw is sometimes the best option.

Circular saw. If you simply can't loosen the fasteners or get at them with a reciprocating saw—or if the board is already damaged—a circular saw will be your best friend. This tool can be indispensible in quickly and accurately cutting deck boards free of overly nailed ends. Adding a fine-tooth finish blade will ensure you make the clean cuts necessary for some of the more delicate and exacting projects in this book.

Nippers. This handy tool is essentially a specialized pair of pliers, effective at pulling nails or, in the case of pallets, nail fragments or cut ends out of wood meant for upcycling projects.

Mini hacksaw. If you're not comfortable with investing in or using a reciprocating saw, this handy little tool can be a great alternative. It's basically a handle that holds a metal-cutting hacksaw, with the blade projecting out beyond on the handle. It's well suited to slipping under a deck board to cut a fastener. It will take more time and elbow grease than a reciprocating saw would, but costs far less and is safer to use.

When deconstructing pallets, it's often wisest to start with the simplest solution and work up from there. If the pallet is not constructed with special nails, a hammer may do the trick. But most pallets are going to require a more substantial solution.

HOW TO DECONSTRUCT A PALLET: FOUR OPTIONS

Where the board ends are already loose or standard nails have been used, a claw hammer can work to separate a deck board. Use another hammer or mallet to secure the claw end under the end of the board as close to the nails as possible, and then carefully lever the board up.

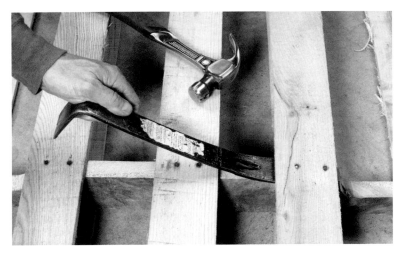

Pry bars have an advantage over claw hammers in their shape. The wide face and gentle curve of the handle combine to spread stress over a wider area, which means less board breakage. Tap the tongue of the bar under one side of the board near the nails and slowly lever the board up a tiny bit. Then work on the other side of the board. Repeat until the board end breaks loose.

To use a pallet buster, simply wedge the tines under the board and lever up even firmly attached boards with ease and a minimum of breakage. However, these justify their cost only when you're deconstructing several pallets.

When other options aren't going to do the trick, slide the moving metal-cutting blade of a reciprocating saw between a board and the stringer or block, quickly severing any fasteners.

SAFETY FIRST

When working with wood taken from a pallet, be careful that there are no hidden fasteners that might cause damage to a saw or injury to the user. Staples, portions of a nail, or other errant pieces of metal can be a danger when working with reclaimed wood. Ensure that the wood you use is free of these by using a lumber metal detector. These handy devices are simple wands that work much like a stud finder; just wave them over the wood and they alert you to any metal—even hidden small pieces of nails.

FINISHING TOUCHES

Although several of the projects shown in this book can be left rough, many will need to be prepped for finishing or final use. Depending on the pallets you're upcycling, the wood may be distressed, presenting splinters and an unpleasant surface to the touch. Some are so rough that you may have to simply accept a more rustic appearance or the fact that you can't smooth them down enough to take a gloss layer of paint. Remember, design flexibility is key when upcycling pallet wood.

A jointer is an effective way to square up pallet boards, giving them clean, sharp edges and flat faces that mate perfectly in projects like the ones in this book. However, a jointer is a fairly expensive piece of woodworking machinery and not every shop has one. In addition, a jointer only works on fairly thick pieces. If you have deconstructed deck boards thinner than three-quarters of an inch, jointing them may not be an option.

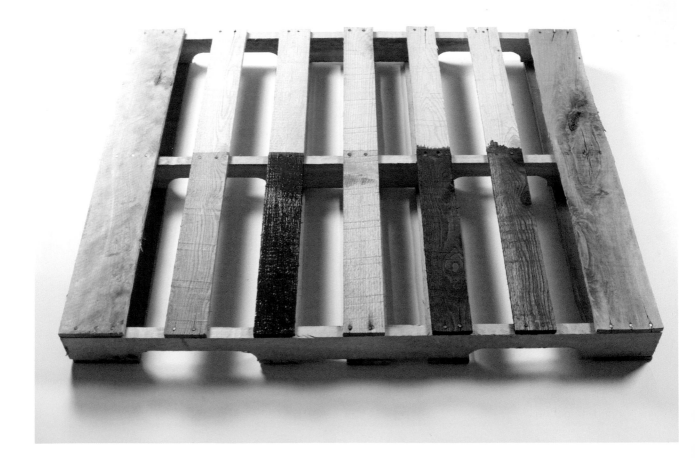

Even if you don't have access to a jointer, you can square off the faces of pallet boards with defects using a table saw; it will just take more careful handling. In either case, you'll need to adjust measurements, because in removing wood to square up members, you'll be altering the actual dimensions of the pieces.

A simple sanding can clean up less serious defects, except where the wood face is so substandard as to be unworkable. In any case, if you're painting or otherwise finishing the final creation, you'll want to sand to prep the surface for the finish.

You can use an old-fashioned sanding block and sheets of sandpaper, but the more efficient solution is a palm sander. These can smooth pallet-wood surfaces quickly and give you far more control than belt or orbital sanders.

Regardless of how you choose to finish your project, first it needs to get built. And that's what the rest of this book is all about.

A palm sander is an ideal way to smooth pallet wood—it's much quicker than a sanding block and gives you much more control than a belt or orbital sander.

FINE FINISHES

Prepping and finishing pallet wood can be your way of giving any pallet-wood project a polished look. It's also your chance to ensure an upscale project gives no clues to its original identity. Just know that some wood you salvage from pallets may not take a finish because of an overly rough or degraded surface.

The challenge is that there isn't just one type of pallet wood. Different manufacturers use different woods. In fact, the same manufacturer may use different woods at different times, depending on availability. Different woods take paint or stains differently (which is why it's always good to do a practice run on a scrap piece of the wood you intend to finish).

Adding to the jumble, different pallets will be rougher or smoother, depending on how and where they were manufactured. They will also be less or more dirty, depending on how old the pallet is and what it was used to carry. That's why preparation is key, no matter what final look you're after.

PREPPING PALLET WOOD

Prepping the wood you've reclaimed from a pallet starts with cleaning. If, in the fabrication process, you already smoothed the edges and faces of the boards, chances are that they won't need to be cleaned. However, if the wood came from a well-traveled pallet that you simply disassembled (or used mostly whole), it may need to be cleaned prior to sanding and prepping.

Soap and water may do the trick for superficial dirt and even mild grease marks. More stubborn stains and grease can be removed with trisodium phosphate (TSP), following the manufacturer's instructions on the box. No matter how you clean the wood, make sure it's absolutely dry before you continue prepping it.

Most finishes require a sanded surface with just enough tooth to allow the finish to absorb into the surface. For pallet wood, that generally means working down from 80-grit to 110- or 120-grit sandpaper. Depending on the size of the project, sand by hand or use a palm sander. Think twice before turning to a belt or orbital sander. Given the mottled shades of some pallet wood, it's easy with these more powerful tools to spend too long on one spot and sand a slope or depression into the surface. This can be a critical error on thinner deck boards, where it can weaken the board beyond use.

If you're planning on using a high-gloss product to finish your project, follow up any sanding with a wipe-down using a slightly damp, lint-free cloth or tack cloth. Even minute particles of dust can ruin a smooth, glossy surface.

A FLAWLESS FINISH

Painting a pallet-wood project isn't much different than painting any other type of wood. Use a quality primer to lay down a good bed for the topcoat. The best brush to use to paint most of the projects in this book is a two-inch chip brush. For flawless gloss surfaces, sand lightly between coats (you can add up to four coats).

If you're staining a project, consider using a stain-and-sealant product to cut down on the work you'll need to do. These formulations offer great coverage and an all-in-one solution. However, whether you're staining or finishing with a combination product, it's wise to test the product on the underside of a board or other inconspicuous area. For the same reason, it's always good to start with a light coat, because it's much easier to darken a stain than it is to lighten it.

For the outdoor projects in this book, a sealant topcoat, such as polyurethane or spar varnish, is a good idea to ensure the longevity of what you build. However, keep in mind that pallet wood was meant for exposure to abuse and the elements, so even unfinished, the wood will usually hold up for a long time.

SPECIAL EFFECTS

If you're after a weathered, aged look with a painted project, skip the primer and let the paint soak into the wood unevenly. You can also lightly sand areas of the wood to erode portions of the paint. As an alternative, use multiple paint colors, sanding away the topcoat to reveal patches of the color underneath.

To distress a surface you'll be staining, beat it lightly with a chain or other implement to create the appearance of timeworn damage. Then stain as you would otherwise.

Sanding is the solution for any project where you want smoother edges on your pallet.

2 YARD & GARDEN PROJECTS

Given its natural weathered appearance and innate durability, pallet wood is ideal for outdoor structures. Not only does the look fit right in with plants, shrubs, and natural surfaces like stone patios (not to mention wood decks!), pallet wood is incredibly tough.

Let the rain, snow, sleet, and hail do their worst. Your pallet planter or birdhouse will be just fine after the storm passes. That's not to say that you have to leave pallet-wood outdoor structures in their natural state—unfinished. Any of these projects certainly look great that way, but you can also stain them, or even paint them, to suit your own outdoor living spaces, landscaping, and personal tastes. The key is to choose those projects that will have the biggest impact and make the most sense given your house and your yard.

A **Porch Swing** (page 40) is a lovely, evocative visual, but not if you don't have a sturdy porch roof (or thick, seventy-year-old tree branch) from which to hang it. If your backyard space is all patio and pavers, a **Patio Loveseat** (page 37) might be the wiser choice. Whatever your requirements and landscaping style, you're sure to find a project here that adds immeasurably to your outdoor fun.

SMALL-BIRD BIRDHOUSE

Unless you have musician neighbors, the prettiest sound you'll hear in your backyard is the call of songbirds. Of course, that means you have to invite them into the yard in the first place, and there's no better invitation than a short-term rental your feathered friends can call their own.

The challenge is that small songbirds will only stay in a residence where they feel safe. If the entry hole and space inside are too large, the songbirds will quickly be evicted by larger, more aggressive birds. And, unfortunately, crows and blue jays aren't known for the pretty sounds they make. That's why this house is sized just right for birds such as starlings or sparrows. Pair the house with a squirrel-proof bird feeder and you may even get songbirds to overwinter in the residence.

The design is fairly plain, but you can spruce it up with paint or decorations to match the look of your yard or garden. Birds won't be put off by unusual color schemes. Just make sure to hang the birdhouse where predators such as cats can't get to it, or the birds will head to more welcoming pastures. In any case, plan on disassembling the birdhouse after a few seasons to clean it out and keep your bird visitors safe from parasites and diseases.

The construction itself is basic and translates to a super-easy woodworking project. Even if your skill level is firmly in the "beginner" camp, you'll find this birdhouse doable. Just keep in mind that a small project such as this is not forgiving of errors; be precise and careful with your measurements and you'll wind up with a yard accent that does justice to the birds and the landscaping in equal measure.

WHAT YOU'LL NEED

Time: **20 minutes** | Difficulty: **Easy**

TOOLS:

Circular saw

Speed square

Measuring tape

Hole saw with 1 ¼" bit

Bar clamps

Power drill and bits

2 ½" paintbrush (optional)

MATERIALS:

1 pallet

100-grit sandpaper

Wood glue

Finish nails

Wood putty

Paint (optional)

Eye screws

Small-gauge chain or paracord

HOW YOU MAKE IT

1. Use the circular saw to cut 1 x 6" end deck boards into two sidewalls 8½" long; a floor 4" long; and front and back walls 11" long. Use a speed square to mark two 45° cuts in one end of each wall to create a peak. Cut the roof pieces 10" long, and rip one down to 4¾" wide.

2. Use a 1¼" hole saw to drill the entry hole in the front wall, 8" up from the bottom and centered side to side.

3. Sand the pieces with 100-grit sandpaper. Make sure the entry hole is smooth.

4. Clamp the floor of the birdhouse to a worktable and align a sidewall in position along one long edge, with the edges flush. Drill pilot holes through the base. Coat the edge of the floor with wood glue and nail the wall to the floor with finish nails. Repeat with the opposite wall.

5. Attach the front and back walls in the same way, edge-gluing the surfaces to one another and drilling pilot holes for the finish nails along the edges.

6. Clamp the shorter roof surface to the worktable and align the longer one along the edge. Drill pilot holes, coat the mating edges with wood glue, and nail the roof together.

7. Set the roof in place on the birdhouse body, centered front to back. Drill pilot holes every 2" along the front and back edges. Coat the mating edges with glue and nail the roof to the walls.

8. Putty over nail heads, sand, and paint as desired. Screw in two eye screws opposite each other on either side of the roof. Hang the birdhouse from a tree limb with small-gauge chain or paracord.

CUSTOMIZING YOUR BIRDHOUSE

This project includes some features that may not be advisable, depending on how you want to use your birdhouse and what birds you're hoping to attract. If you want to guarantee the longevity of your birdhouse, you may want to substitute galvanized screws for the finish nails used here.

The birdhouse also makes use of a one-and-one-quarter-inch entry hole, but some birds prefer different size holes. The chart below provides measurements for common birds you may be looking to attract.

Bird	Hole Size	Placement Height from Ground
Eastern Bluebird	1 ½"	8' high, in open area
Tree Swallow	1"	6-8' high, in open area
Purple Martin	2 ⅛"	20' high
Tufted Titmouse	1 ¼"	8-10' high
Chickadee	1 ⅛"	6-8' high
Nuthatch	1 ¼"	20-25' high
Wren	1"	8-10' high

Also be aware that placement of the house will affect whether birds will use it. Aside from the height recommended above, keep birdhouses away from thick shrubs or branch growth that could serve as concealment of access to the birdhouse for a predator such as a cat. It's ideal to maintain a clear line of sight around the birdhouse, wherever it is hung or mounted on a post, wall, or tree.

SMALL PLANTER

A standalone planter is one of the most useful additions to any yard, garden, deck, or patio. The portability of a planter such as this one means you can move sensitive trees or shrubs inside or out, depending on the weather. It also allows you to give the plant exactly the amount of sun it needs, or put edible container plants where they'll be most accessible.

Although this is a small planter, it will accommodate many different plants, from a rhododendron to a miniature rosebush to a tree such as a crepe myrtle. One of the wonderful things about planter culture is that you control watering and soil, so that you can plant your ornamental in the richest, most nutritious loam possible, with just the right acid balance to keep it healthy and thriving. The control over environment also means you can adjust the soil to grow fussy, high-maintenance plants that might otherwise be impossible to nurture in your garden.

The planter itself is easy to build. The design is entirely scalable and straightforward, with a minimum of cutting and fabrication. You can customize the look with different color paints (don't paint or finish the interior), stains, or clear finishes. If you decide to paint the planter in a color, make sure the hue you've chosen blends well with the house and landscaping, or the look will grow old and dated very quickly. In most cases, it's usually best to leave the planter unfinished.

You can, however, dress up your planter in other ways. Simple stencils are a great decoration that adds visual interest to the planter. Metal straps can also create a distinctive look. For instance, line the top or bottom trim—or both—with copper bands. The copper will age into a fetching matte green patina that blends seamlessly with the look of the wood.

WHAT YOU'LL NEED

Time: **30 minutes** | Difficulty: **Easy**

TOOLS:

Circular saw or table saw

Measuring tape

Metal framing square

Power drill and bits

Staple gun

Palm sander or sanding block

Paintbrush (optional)

MATERIALS:

2 pallets

2" nails

3" wood screws

Landscape fabric

2" wood screws

80-grit sandpaper

Wood putty

Paint or finish (optional)

HOW YOU MAKE IT

1. Cut eight side panels 20" long and eight side panels 17½" long, from deck boards. Cut eight corner trim pieces 16" long, from deck boards.

2. Assemble the planter side panels on a flat, level work surface. Align two trim pieces, vertical and parallel, spaced about 12" apart. Stack four panels of the same length in a column, face down on the trim pieces. The top edge of the top panel should be flush to the top of the trim pieces. Use a framing

PLANTER BOX PARTNERS

Sure, it can be just a simple home for a plant, but this planter can also be paired with a number of structures to make the most of its potential. These include add-ons that serve a purely aesthetic purpose and more useful complements that increase the type of plants you can grow. Choose the one that makes the most sense for your garden and preferences.

• **The Unplanted Planter.** You don't necessarily have to go to the trouble of lining and planting the planter. You can opt for the quick-switch option of seasonal flowering plants or plants already at home in a container by simply placing the container in the planter. For short pots and other shallow containers, place bolsters made from scraps of pallet wood under the pot so that the top of the lip sits about even with the top of the planter (make sure the drainage holes in the container are not blocked). If you want to maintain the illusion of a planted planter, top the container with tufts of peat or coir, and fill the spaces between the container and the inside surfaces of the planter with the material.

• **The Planter Cold Frame.** Cold frames are popular for avid gardeners who want to keep their edible gardens growing into the winter. You can use the same idea with this planter. Remove the soil halfway down the planter and plant it with lettuces, herbs, or other low-growing edibles. Add a simple thermometer inside, right above the soil. Then, when the cold weather hits, cover the top with an old window, a sheet of Plexiglas, or a even a sheet of six-mil plastic sheeting held in place with rocks or bricks around the lip of the planter. If you're feeling ambitious, you can build a simple frame from pallet-wood scraps to hold the window material. Either way, keep an eye on the growing edibles, because the cold frame will most likely need to be vented as the temperature rises in the direct midday sun, to keep the plants from wilting.

• **Trellised to Impress.** A trellis can be a beautiful complement to a wood planter—one that opens up the type and species of plants you can grow. A simple trellis attached to one side of the planter will support climbing or sprawling plants and can create a green wall. For even more impressive eye candy, install a corner trellis, and tuck the planter into the inside corner of a house or patio.

square to check that the panels are perfectly aligned.

3. Adjust the trim pieces so that they protrude exactly the width of one of your deck boards on each side (use a scrap piece of deck board as a spacer). Nail the panels to the trim with two nails per end.

4. Repeat the process to build the remaining walls. Position one short wall against the inside edge of one long wall to create one corner of the planter. Drill 4 pilot holes spaced evenly down each trim piece and screw the panels together with 3" wood screws. Repeat with the remaining walls to construct the box of the planter.

5. Measure the exact width of the bottom at three places along the inside of the box (it should be 17½"). Cut the bottom boards from stringers, to fit. Screw the four floorboards in place, spaced evenly, with 3" wood screws. Drill ⅛" holes in a random pattern in the floorboards, for drainage.

6. Line the inside of the box with landscape fabric, cut and doubled over as necessary, and stapled to the walls. The fabric should create a tight pocket for the dirt.

7. Cut the top frame pieces 23" long, from deck boards. Miter the ends 45°, and dry fit the frame to the top of the box. Drill pilot holes down into the trim and walls, and attach the frame with 2" wood screws. (If the deck boards you're using are less than ¾" thick, you may need to use 1 × 1" cleats—cut from stringer waste material—to create a holding surface for the top frame.)

8. Cover the screw heads with wood putty, let dry, and sand the planter smooth. Paint or finish the planter as desired. Position the planter in its final location. Fill it with potting soil and your preferred plant.

THE VEGETABLE PLANTER

When most people think of small patio planters, they envision a lovely ornamental tree or bush—basically outdoor decoration. But while this planter can certainly host the elegant lace-leaf Japanese maple or perky mock orange tree, the possibilities are much more diverse. A small planter such as the one in this project can be perfect for growing your favorite edibles. That doesn't mean you necessarily have to sacrifice beauty; many edible plants (think the bold colors of rainbow chard) provide stunning visuals in addition to nutritious dinner side dishes. Don't be afraid to experiment, because, given that most edible plants are essentially annuals, you'll have plenty of chances to switch up the look and crops you grow. Here's a list of some of the simplest and most rewarding veggies to grow in this planter.

The beautiful purple blooms of chives add an eye-catching feature to this rough planter crafted from unnotched stringers. The planter holds a small kitchen herb garden that is conveniently located a few steps from the backdoor of the kitchen.

• **Tomatoes.** The size of this planter is ideal for a single tomato plant. The self-contained planter culture ensures you can give the tomatoes exactly the amount of water they need to become beautiful and delicious. Grow heirloom, hybrid, or even cherry tomatoes, as you prefer. Just be sure to add support, such as a tomato cage, to allow for the best air circulation and to support heavy mature fruit so that it doesn't damage the plant. Tuck in marigolds around the tomato plant and you'll deter some insects from bothering it.

• **Rosemary.** This tough perennial provides you with all the herb you can use year to year and doesn't require much in return. The plant also offers tiny, lovely blue flowers and a fragrance that is a welcome addition to any patio.

• **Cabbage.** A single planter can be a wonderful location for a cabbage plant, allowing it plenty of room to grow and lots of air circulation that will keep pests and diseases at bay. Ornamental cabbage offers beautiful cold-weather colors and forms.

• **Beets, carrots, and other root crops.** These crops may not seem natural choices for a container, but they grow well in the confines of a planter, and the greens of root crops like these offer eye-catching foliage.

• **Peppers.** Bell peppers grow on a handsome plant with a form that perfectly complements a planter. However, for the most visual bang for your buck, let them mature into colored peppers, or grow multicolored hot peppers in the planter.

• **Greens.** For a foliage-only display, consider growing cut-and-come-again greens such as lettuce, spinach, or—if you want a spectacular visual display—rainbow chard. You can also plant beets for their greens and enjoy a two-for-one bounty.

RAISED BED

Want to give your vegetables the best chance to not only survive, but thrive? Want to cut down on the backache of weeding? Want to keep your garden tidy and easy to manage? Well, look no further. Turn to raised-bed gardening.

A raised bed like the one in this project is the perfect home for your plants. The contained structure allows you to create the absolutely ideal soil mix for whatever edibles you choose to grow. A raised bed warms much earlier in spring, allowing you to get a jump on your gardening. It also gives you an amazing amount of control over the plants as they grow.

Because the plants are elevated, it's easier to inspect them and detect and head off any pest or disease problems early. A raised bed also ensures proper drainage, so that your plants get just the moisture they need. The bed can be used to create a barrier to creepy-crawlies, such as slugs and snails, who are out to eat your plants before you have a chance to harvest them. Because you garden from the edges, a raised bed is also a way to combat soil compaction. Loose soil is easier to tend and better for plant roots.

This bed is roughly seven inches deep, which will accommodate most garden edibles—from a kitchen herb garden to a few square feet of tomatoes. If you want to grow crops that require a deeper bed, such as potatoes, just add pallets on top, in the same way you build the base. Properly planned out, planted, and tended, a single raised bed like this one can produce enough summer vegetables to feed a family of four. And it's easy enough to add beds as you see fit—you'll find them easier to work than a traditional row garden.

A raised bed is also a good-looking addition to a yard or garden and can even create a growing space on a concrete patio or gravel side yard. You can paint the outside to suit your tastes or to match a house or fence. Leave the beds natural for a rustic appeal or just to limit the amount of work you'll have to do. Just make sure that no toxic finishes are used on the inside of the box.

RAISED BEDS SQUARE FOOT BY SQUARE FOOT

A raised bed is the cornerstone of the widespread popular gardening movement, Square Foot Gardening. This system uses a square raised bed that measures four feet by four feet to create sixteen square feet, each of which is planted with a different edible. You can adapt the raised bed here for Square Foot Gardening by simply adjusting to four ten-inch "feet." The bed is divided, as with any Square Foot Garden, into individual square feet with the help of a wood, twine, or plastic "grid." Then the seeds are planted according to the precise spacing of the Square Foot Gardening system (using far fewer seeds than traditional gardening). To learn more about how to plant your own Square Foot Garden, pick up a copy of *All New Square Foot Gardening: The Revolutionary Way to Grow More In Less Space*, by Mel Bartholomew.

The Square Foot Gardening system relies on a wood, plastic, or twine grid that marks off the squares, each of which are to be planted with a different edible.

WHAT YOU'LL NEED

Time: **30 minutes** | Difficulty: **Easy**

TOOLS:

Pry bar or hammer

Power drill and screwdriver bit

Circular saw

Measuring tape

Staple gun and staples

MATERIALS:

2 pallets

4" wood screws

3" wood screws

2" wood screws

Landscape fabric

Topsoil or potting soil

HOW YOU MAKE IT

1. Use a pry bar or hammer to strip the bottom deck boards from 2 pallets. Remove the top deck boards, leaving only the deck boards at either end.

2. Clear a section of lawn or bare dirt and level it. Set one of the pallets upside down (deck-board side on the ground).

3. Set the other pallet on top of the first one, deck-board side up, with the stringers aligned. The notches should mate, forming oval openings on each side.

4. Use 4" screws to screw the top stringers to the bottom stringers toenail style, driving the screws through the end of the top stringers.

5. Screw deck boards to the stringer ends with 3" wood screws, to enclose the open ends of the pallets. Measure and cut gusset plates from 6"-wide deck boards, to be placed on the inside of each bed side between the stringer cutouts. Screw the gusset plates in place with 2" wood screws.

6. Cut 12"-long (or long enough to cover the cutouts on your stringers) faceplates from deck boards to cover the notch openings in the side stringers. Screw the plates over the openings with 2" wood screws.

7. Line the two cavities on either side of the central stringers with landscape fabric, stapling it to the stringers. Fill the planter with topsoil or potting soil, and begin planting your raised bed garden.

RULES FOR RAISED BEDS

The secret to growing the best garden possible in raised beds is accessibility. A few basic rules will help you optimize your pallet raised bed—especially if you choose to grow more than one.

• Plan your placement carefully. A raised bed such as the one in this project is difficult, if not impossible, to move once it's filled with soil and plants. Observe the sun and shade patterns in your yard, and settle on the perfect spot for the raised bed. If you're growing taller plants such as corn, make sure there is some sort of wind break to protect the plants when they are mature. Grow taller plants in the bed on the south side, so that they don't shade other plants.

• Leave at least four feet between raised beds to allow for maximum access. Remember, not only do you need room to work and move around the beds, you'll probably also need to manipulate equipment such as buckets, watering cans, or even a wheelbarrow in the aisles between beds.

• Minimize weeds with a base barrier. By using a blocking barrier, such as the landscape fabric in this project, you ensure that your raised bed will be weed-free. You can substitute black plastic sheeting or a similar material.

• Run drip irrigation whenever possible. It's usually an easy task to route drip lines through a raised bed, and it's preferable to watering with a watering can or even a hose. Drip lines save water, ensure your plants get exactly the moisture they need, and are trouble-free for the gardener.

• Protect the plants as necessary. It's easy to make a fence of chicken wire wrapped around tall posts made from ripped-down deck boards and nailed onto the outside of the raised bed's corners. A simple fence like this will keep your tasty veggies safe from deer and other hungry wildlife, not to mention family pets.

The beauty of a pallet raised bed is that it can be put on any flat surface, which includes a temporary gardening table (even the table can be made from pallets or pallet wood) that raises the bed up so that a person with disabilities can garden. This can be a wonderful solution for older or infirm gardeners who simply can't endure the stresses and strains of kneeling for long periods.

PATIO LOVESEAT

Let's face it; patio furniture is downright expensive. Even cheap plastic versions aren't all that cheap. The investment is even more galling when you consider how short the lifespan of patio furniture can be, given relentless exposure to bright sunlight and the elements.

The answer? Build your own nearly free outdoor seating.

Although it might not be the first option that pops to mind, pallet wood is a fantastic material for creating extremely durable, comfortable, and low-cost outdoor furnishings. Think about it. Not only do you want your patio furniture to hold up to day after day of harsh sunlight, but it also needs to tolerate the occasional downpour. Of course, it also has to handle the rough-and-tumble of a neighborhood cookout or kids and pets having fun outside. Build patio or deck furnishings out of pallets, and you're using wood that was originally selected for its incredible strength, resilience, and durability.

This loveseat is a perfect example of the kind of extraordinary outdoor fixture pallets can become. It will endure not only the elements, but also food and drink spills as well as rambunctious relatives and youngsters. It's small enough to fit even a tiny townhouse patio and comfortable enough to spend hours in.

This is such a cozy seating option that you may want to pair it with the **Adirondack Chair** on page 52 to create a seating group around a fire pit. With fun, handsome, and durable seating like this waiting outside your backdoor, you may even find yourself spending more time outside the house than in it.

HOW YOU MAKE IT

1. Remove the deck boards from the bottom of a pallet. Set the pallet on a clean, flat, level work surface (the ends of the stringers will be pointing to the front). Set another pallet on top. The stringers should be aligned and the pallets should be flush side to side and front to back. Stringer notches, if any, should all be facing down.

2. Bar-clamp the panels. Screw the pallets together by driving 4" wood screws down at an angle through the ends of the top stringers and into the top edges of the stringers below. Screw the end deck boards together with 1½" wood screws, using four per side.

3. Remove one end deck board from the top of a third pallet. Place it on top of the two base pallets. Screw it to the pallet below, in the same way you joined the lower two pallets.

4. Nail two deck boards across the front ends of the stringers with 2" finish nails, to form a fascia on the front of the loveseat.

5. Remove the deck boards from the bottom of a pallet. Cut the stringers 25" long, removing a top deck board as necessary to make the cut. This will form the back of the

CREATIVE OPTIONS FOR PATIO LOVESEATS

Although the design of the patio loveseat is meant to be both compact and attractive, you can customize your loveseat to better suit the dimensions and features of your yard.

Convert to perimeter seating for small yards. Remove the back from this loveseat and the base can be attached directly to fencing around the outside of a small yard, to take up the smallest footprint while still offering plenty of seating. Screw the base directly to wood or plastic fencing; drill holes in the base and wire it to cyclone or steel wire fencing.

Exploit large outdoor areas by using multiples of the loveseat. This design doesn't include arms, which makes it easy to join multiple loveseats into a large seating structure that might work better in a long narrow yard or just to border one edge of a large patio or deck.

Go poolside by lowering the loveseat. Omit the bottom layer of pallets for the seat to put this loveseat on the level of a chaise lounge and adapt it for use next to a pool.

Capture it between large plants in a dense garden. The loveseat is just as usable in a setting where it will serve as a standalone bench. Blend it into a thoughtfully designed ornamental garden by positioning it next to a path and put planters on either side with tall or bushy growing shrubs or ornamental trees.

loveseat. Use a speed square and pencil to mark a 15° angle on the face of each stringer at the cut end. Use a circular saw to make the angle cuts.

6. Enlist a helper to place the seatback in position, with the cut stringer ends sitting flush on the exposed stringers of the top pallet. Drill angled holes through the edges of the back's stringers, down into the top of the seat stringers. Countersink the holes and fasten the back to the top seat pallet with 6" lag screws.

7. Sand the loveseat all over. Remove any splinters and smooth any rough sections. Paint or stain the loveseat if desired, or leave it natural to blend with the landscaping. Make the loveseat more comfortable by adding seat and back cushions.

6

PORCH SWING

Nothing brings to mind the lazy days of late summer quite like a porch swing. It's really an invitation to slowly move back and forth, a cold glass of lemonade in your hand and nothing on your mind. A porch swing can be a sanctuary away from the hectic pace of everyday life, the perfect way to unplug and unwind. Of course, first you have to build it.

The structure of a pallet lends itself well to the stresses and strains of a hanging piece of furniture. The wood is also durable in the face of the summer thunderstorm that blows water onto the porch and over the swing. It also resists the occasional bit of dropped food or spilled iced tea during those slow, informal dinners on the porch.

This swing can be a great way to exploit an otherwise dead corner of the porch—just make sure you leave plenty of room for the swing's modest arc, so that it doesn't hit any house walls or, even worse, windows. Always leave at least four feet in front of and behind the swing for the swing arc.

More importantly, only hang the swing from strong structural members that can bear the weight. Not only is the swing heavy itself, it becomes all the more so with two adults sitting side by side. As long as the supporting structure overhead is secure, the swing itself will easily support two healthy adults.

For that same reason, this project was hung by chains rather than more attractive rope. Heavy-duty chain is a must if you want to ensure the swing is as safe as it is alluring.

WHAT YOU'LL NEED

Time: **1 hour** | Difficulty: **Medium**

TOOLS:

Measuring tape
Speed square
Carpenter's pencil
Jigsaw or reciprocating saw
Power drill and bits
Circular saw or table saw
Palm sander

Paintbrush (optional)

MATERIALS:

2 pallets
5" wood screws
6" FastenMaster HeadLok screws
(4) 3" wood screws

(6) $5/16$x4" lag eye bolts
(12) $1/4$ x 4" lag eye screws
(4) $1/4$" carbon steel quick link
$3/16$" grade 30 zinc-plated chain
80- and 100-grit sandpaper
Paint (optional)
Seat and back cushions (optional)

HOW YOU MAKE IT

1. Measure and mark the faces of a pallet's stringers with a speed square, for a 15° cut 28" from one end of the pallet. The cut should be angled down toward the back. Make the cuts with a reciprocating saw, and then square off the angle cuts of the larger section (the seat).

2. Sit the cut edges of the smaller section's (the seatback) stringers on the top edges of the seat's stringers. (You may have to remove the rearmost board on the seat so that back's stringer ends can sit flush on top of the seat's stringers.)

3. Screw the back to the seat with 5" wood screws driven from each side of the seatback's stringers, down into the seat's stringers.

4. Carefully place the swing upside down and drive 6" HeadLok screws through the bottom edges of the seat stringers up into the back stringers.

5. Hold a deconstructed stringer diagonally across the outer faces of the seat and back, as an arm. Mark angled cuts on each end of the stringer. Make the cuts with a circular saw. Use the arm as a template to mark and cut a stringer for the opposite arm.

6. Screw the arms to the seat and back with two 3" wood screws per end, driven off center. Drill starter holes for the lag eye bolts in the arm where they overlap the seat and back stringer faces. Screw in the bolts as tightly as possible.

7. Measure the on-center spacing of the porch roof joists and cut two stringer scraps to span three joists. Face-screw these braces above where you want the swing, spaced on center equal to the outside width of the swing. Use two ¼ x 4" lag screws at each joist. Drill a

starter hole and screw a lag eye screw up through each brace into the center joist.

8. Use a carbon steel quick link on each side to hang 4' sections of ³⁄₁₆"-grade 30 zinc-plated chain (you may need to adjust the chain lengths; the swing should hang 17" above the floor).

9. Sit the swing on supports 17" off the floor, and tilt it to the desired final angle. Measure from each lag eye screw to the end of the chain hanging from the roof and cut chains to those lengths.

10. Sand the surface of the swing and finish as desired. Attach the support chains to the swing's lag eye screws with quick links, and join the free ends to the roof chain with quick links. Add a seat and back cushions for comfort as desired.

HANGING PORCH SWINGS

Securely hanging a porch swing is crucial to prevent personal injury or damage to your porch and home. It's always best to err on the side of overkill when it comes to supporting large amounts of weight from a home's load-bearing structure.

To guarantee the integrity of the chain support, use a screw eye with at least a four-inch shaft. You can make installing a screw eye directly into a joist easier by drilling a pilot hole a size or two smaller than the screw eye shaft. Tighten the screw eye down by sticking a large screwdriver through the eye and slowly turning it clockwise.

If you don't have a porch, you may be tempted to hang the swing from a large, old-growth tree. This is usually not advisable because there is no way to assess the internal integrity of a tree branch, and the outer end remains unsupported. If you do decide to hang the swing from a tree,

One of the most stable ways to secure a porch swing to a porch ceiling is with cross braces running perpendicular to the roof joists, as shown here.

the branch must be at least eight inches in diameter, live rather than dead, with no visible damage, defects, or disease. The branch should be growing upward rather than parallel to the ground. As with porch joists, you should use a chain to hang the swing, but be aware that the chain will damage the tree over time.

CHAISE LOUNGE

This project builds on the features that make the chaise lounge a classic piece of outdoor furniture. The length ensures that even tall people can stretch out, and the adjustable back means that the lounge is adaptable—it can be a handy put-your-legs-up place to read the morning paper and then become a nice tanning bed in the afternoon.

As with all outdoor pallet furniture, thoroughly sand all surfaces. A splintery edge can ruin any sun-drenched afternoon. No matter where you put the chaise, you'll want it looking its best. You can paint it if you prefer, but chaise lounges are traditionally finished natural or lightly stained—a waterproof finish is ideal, especially one with added UV protection. For maximum comfort, you'll also want to add a cushion.

WHAT YOU'LL NEED

Time: **1.5 hours** | Difficulty: **Hard**

TOOLS:

Circular saw
Measuring tape
Carpenter's pencil
Power drill and bits
1" spade bit
Palm sander
Paintbrush (optional)

MATERIALS:

3 pallets
Construction adhesive or waterproof wood glue
2 ½" wood screws
3" wood screws
4" wood screws
2" wood screws

(2) 1 ½ x 3" stainless-steel marine butt hinges
1 x 34" metal dowel
Sandpaper
Paint or finish (optional)
Cushion (optional)

HOW YOU MAKE IT

1. Remove the bottom deck boards from two pallets. Cut the top deck boards of both flush with one edge of the center stringer (the seat and back are both 24¾" wide, with two stringers and deck boards running flush to each side).

2. Measure and mark the stringers 46" long for the seat and 30" long for the back. Remove any deck boards that would be in the way as you make the cuts. Cut the seat and back to length. Cut two frame rails 40" long and two 36" long from deck boards (one short and one long rail will be joined to make each side frame).

3. Cut five cleats from stringers, equal to the inside width of the stringers in the pallet section you cut. Construct the double cleat by coating one face of a cleat with construction adhesive (or use waterproof wood glue) and mating a second cleat to it flush all around. Screw them together with rows of 2 ½" wood screws staggered every 4 inches.

4. Line the cleats up in a row, parallel to each other, on a flat, level, clean work surface. Lay a long and a short rail board on their faces, running together on each side of the cleats. They should be perpendicular to the cleats.

5. Position two cleats 2" in from each end of the rails. Position a third 20" from the front edge of the long rail boards. Position the double cleat bridging the butt joint between the two rail sections on each side. Mark the cleat locations on each rail board. Measure to check that the cleat marks are exactly the same on each side.

6. Flip the rail boards on one side up so that they are face to end with the cleats and so

that the bottom edges of the rails are flush with the bottom faces of the cleats. Drill pilot holes and screw the rail boards to the cleats with two 3" wood screws per cleat (use four screws for the center double cleat). Repeat with the opposite side to complete the frame.

7. Cut six legs 7¾" long, from stringers. Cut a 1 ¾" square notch in one corner of each leg (measure the cleat widths first and adjust as necessary). Attach the legs to the rails with the notches butted to the inside edges of

the front and back cleats and the back edge of the double cleat. Screw the rails to the legs with 2" wood screws and the legs to the cleats by driving 4" wood screws down through the cleats and into the leg tops.

8. Notch the seat frame to sit over the top of the doubled-up frame cleat. Sit the top sections in place on the cleats, adjusting their position to line them up with the frame. Screw the rails to the seat stringers with 2" wood screws.

9. Remove deck boards as necessary to allow for placement of the hinge flanges on the cut ends of the seat and back stringers. Rip deck boards as necessary and screw them into gaps to make a fairly uniform seat and back surface. (If your stringers have notches, sister unnotched waste sections over the notches to create a flat surface flush with the bottom of the stringer, so that the back sits properly on the prop adjustment.) Screw down the hinges between seat and back stringers using $1\frac{1}{2} \times 3$" stainless-steel marine butt hinges (or substitute standard 4" strap hinges by the width of your stringers).

10. With the back in the upright position, measure and mark the rails on each side for the back adjustment holes, every 4" starting 4" back from the hinge location. Drill 1" holes at the marks, 1" down from the top of the rails, using a spade bit. Slide a 1 x 34" metal rod through an adjustment hole and set the back against the dowel.

11. Sand the chaise lounge all over and finish with stain, clear finish, or paint, as desired.

QUICK 3

Garden accents are the icing on the cake when it comes to landscaping. Although they are small in stature, they can bring a great big design bang to your outdoor areas. Pallet-wood creations offer quite a bit of flexibility, because the surface appearance is adaptable to a wide range of landscape and garden styles. You can finish any of the projects below to make each distinctive and stand out. Paint plant markers in bright colors and they become interesting visuals in their own right. Distress a pallet trellis and it provides a fascinating foil to the leaves and flowers of climbing plants. As long as the pallet wood is free, experiment to your heart's delight; you've really got nothing to lose. Because all three of these projects are portable, they can easily be hidden from view or placed front and center, as you prefer. Just don't let the interesting appearances fool you; all three of these outdoor additions serve very useful purposes, from marking where plants are to illuminating the garden at night.

1. PALLET PLANT MARKERS

Accent a wonderful country garden with some simple plant markers that will help you and the other gardeners in your family identify exactly what was planted where. These markers are simple to craft from any pallet deck boards. Cut a board in half and rip it lengthwise in half to create the rough shapes. Cut one end of each marker to a stake point to finish the shape.

Embellish the marker as you prefer, by using a jigsaw to cut a curve or other decorative flourish in the top. Hand-letter or stencil letters to create the names of plants and provide an eye-catching graphic in your yard. You can use the markers as purely informative devices, to keep track of what has been planted where, or you can leverage the look as a design feature by painting or staining the markers and using elaborate font stencils for the letters.

2. OUTDOOR LIGHTING FIXTURES

Bring a romantic touch to an outdoor sitting area or secluded corner of the yard by illuminating the space with the soft glow of votive candles in mason jars. Cut a section of a pallet sized to meet your needs; you can also use a whole pallet if you want a lot of light. Remove all but a couple boards on the bottom. Punch holes in the jar lids of four to six Mason jars. Screw small eye screws into the center of each lid (or devise your own hanging hardware solution, such as wrapping the neck of the jar in stripped wire, screwing the lid down over the wire, and hanging the jar from the ends). Screw matching eye screws into the pallet's top deck boards for each one of the Mason jars. A regular pattern is usually the most attractive. Finish the pallet as you prefer (it's usually best to either leave it natural or stain it in a shade that blends with the surroundings). Screw sturdy ceiling hooks into the stringers of the pallet and hang it from a tree branch with chain or rope, or attach it directly to the overhang of a pergola or arbor. Hang the jars by wire if that's what you used to secure the jars, or use small-gauge chains run between the eye screw in the jar lids and the corresponding eye screw in the pallet. In either case, unscrew the lid from each jar, set a votive candle inside, light it, and let the nighttime magic begin.

3. GARDEN TRELLIS

Because of the spaces between deck boards, a pallet can make an ideal garden trellis. Not only is there a lot of surface area for growing plants to be tied to or weave around, the gaps allow for air circulation, which in turn helps combat disease. One of the easiest structures to make from whole pallets is a sandwich-board trellis. Simply remove the bottom boards from two pallets, and lean them together to form an inverted V. Nail one of the removed deck boards horizontally between the outside faces of the stringers on either side. Then just plunk the trellis down wherever you need it and train just about any vining or sprawling plant to grow up the trellis—from zucchinis to cucumbers, and even watermelon! Keep in mind that this sturdy trellis can support even the heaviest fruiting vines. You can craft other types of trellises as well. Cut the boards along one edge of the inside stringer on a pallet to make a long, narrow trellis that would be excellent for climbing roses or vining edibles. Remove two boards at one end and dig postholes for the exposed stringer ends. Then stand the trellis in the holes, firm around the stringer ends, and you have a self-standing trellis exactly where you need it. Of course, you can also attach it to a fence, wall, or the back side of a planter to support plants in different situations. Tie the plants to the deck boards as they grow, or weave them in and out of the gaps between boards.

PLANTER BENCH

The planter bench is a garden furniture hybrid that continues to grow in popularity. That's because it does double duty, with each part of the structure making the other more enjoyable.

This version includes planters on both sides of the bench. The supports for the bench itself are actually built into the walls of the planters on each side. That gives the structure an appealing symmetry and makes it ideal for just about anywhere you need outdoor seating—from a deck to a patio to a shady spot along a garden pathway.

Although the finished project is a spectacular and useful piece of outdoor furniture, it does require attention to detail. Be careful with all the measurements (remember: "measure twice, cut once"), and pay attention to the fine points of how the bench is integrated into the construction of the planters.

The bench is large enough for two people to sit side by side comfortably. The planters can accommodate many different plants and are large enough to support even small ornamental trees such as a mock orange. For a really powerful first impression, plant perfumed plants such as fragrant roses, rosemary, sage, or jasmine. You can also grow vining plants by adding a trellis. Just keep in mind that whatever you plant should not encroach upon the sitting area of the bench, or the bench won't be inviting.

The planter bench looks best left unfinished, so that it weathers to a lovely gray, or finished in a light stain or clear polyurethane. Depending on where you use it, and whether you're going to add sprawling plants to the planters (which will tumble over the sides and partially hide the planters), you can use extremely rough planter wood.

PLANTER BENCH STRATEGIES

There are many ways to build on or optimize the basic idea of this planter bench. Here are a few, but you're sure to come up with some on your own.

• **Extend, extend, extend.** The technique used in this project to integrate the bench in the inner wall of each planter can be replicated to add a bench on the opposite sides of the planters—making a long run of seating ideal for bordering a wall or fence in a long, narrow garden. You can also integrate a bench into the perpendicular planter wall, to make a pair of benches and three planters to go into the corner of a patio or deck.

• **Add a cushion.** Although the look of the bench is most traditional when left bare, a cushion would make the bench more comfortable for extended periods of sitting. This is especially useful if an elderly or infirm person will be tending the planters on each side.

• **Plan for water.** When you're picking out the location of your planter bench unit, it's wise to think about how you'll be watering the plants. Ideally, situate the unit near a garden bed from which you can extend drip irrigation into the planters. That way, the plants in the planters will require little or no maintenance, making this an even more enjoyable garden structure.

WHAT YOU'LL NEED

Time: **2 hours** | Difficulty: **Hard**

TOOLS:

Pry bar or hammer
Power drill and bits
Circular saw or table saw
4 F-style clamps
Palm sander
Staple gun

MATERIALS:

3 pallets
3" finish nails
2" wood screws
3" wood screws
80- and 100-grit sandpaper
Clear finish (optional)
Landscape fabric

HOW YOU MAKE IT

1. Deconstruct three pallets. Build the seat frame using two unnotched stringers (or two clear 2×4s if your stringers are notched), and two 14½" cleats cut from separate stringers. Create the box frame with the cleats running between the rails at either end.

2. Cut ten seat slats 17½" long from deck boards (if your deck boards are thin, you might consider using true 1×4s for added strength). Space the slats out evenly across the tops of the stringer rails. Drill pilot holes and nail the slats to the rails with two finish nails at each end of each board.

3. Cut forty 18"-long panel boards from deck boards. Build the planters' front and back panels by laying two 22"

trim pieces cut from stringers (so that any notches are centered along the length of the trim pieces) parallel on a clean, level work surface. (Adjust your measurements if your stringers are not 1½" thick or your deck boards are not ¾" thick—those are the measurements on which these dimensions are based.) Lay five panel boards across the trim pieces and adjust so that the top and bottom edges are all flush and the trim overhangs the panel boards 2¼" on each side. Screw the panel boards to the trim using 2" wood screws.

4. Construct the two outside planter panels by repeating the process with 17½" trim boards and no overhang.

5. Partially construct the planters by screwing a front and back panel to an outside panel by drilling pilot holes and driving 3" wood screws through the top and bottom trim pieces where they overlap.

6. Attach the inside panel bottom trim to the partially constructed boxes with the panels upright. Use four F-style clamps to hold the bench in position as you drill pilot holes and screw the top front and back panel trim to the side of the seat rails with 3" wood screws. The top of the seat should be flush with the top of the boxes. Repeat with the opposite side.

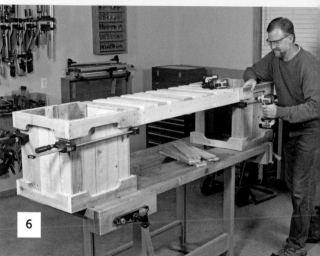

7. Use 2" wood screws to attach the five panel boards vertically to the bench end and inside panel bottom trim. Repeat for the opposite planter.

8. Cut four back and front panel caps 22" long from deck boards (adjust as necessary if your stringers and deck boards are thinner than 1½" and ¾"). Cut four side-panel caps 20½" long (we used 2×4s here). Cut 45° miters in all cap ends.

9. Clamp the caps together on a work surface, and drill pilot holes through the miters (if your deck boards are thin, pocket screw the joints together). Nail the miter joints together with finish nails to construct the cap frames. Center the cap frames on the top of each planter, drill pilot holes, and nail the caps down to the trim.

10. Sand the bench and planter thoroughly. Stain, paint, or finish the structure with a clear finish. Line the inside of each planter with landscape fabric folded and stapled so that it is flush to the panels. Fill the planters with dirt and plant shrubs, miniature trees, or your favorite flowering perennials.

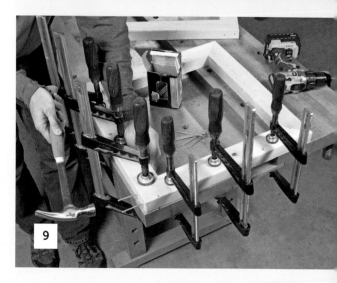

ADIRONDACK CHAIR

The iconic design of this chair can trace its roots back a century, but the look—and, more importantly, the comfort—of this classic chair is timeless. It features an alluring combination of a perfectly slanted back with wide arms that invite relaxation. Even without a cushion, the chair is remarkably comfortable. You can spend hours in one without ever becoming stiff.

The version in this project is fairly easy to construct thanks to some crafting shortcuts. The design is also forgiving of slight mistakes. With a couple of cuts, you can easily change the angle of the recline and the angle of the legs, if they are not to your liking.

The look of the finished chair fits right in with other outdoor furniture, complementing **Chaise Lounges** (page 44), more conventional patio chairs, and even brick benches. The chair is also lightweight enough to be relatively portable. Use it on the deck for casual conversations over a drink with friends, and then move it to the far reaches of the yard for a private weekend reading session.

Don't worry about jostling it as you move it around—the construction is durable and resilient, even in the face of spills, weather, and the occasional sprinkler soaking.

WHAT YOU'LL NEED

Time: **1 hour** | Difficulty: **Medium**

TOOLS:

Circular saw or table saw
Power drill and bits
Measuring tape
Carpenter's pencil
Jigsaw
Carpenter's square
Level
Palm sander
Paintbrush

MATERIALS:

2 pallets
2" wood screws
1 ½" wood screws
3" wood screws
Trammel compass
Finish nails
Wood putty
80- and 100-grit sandpaper
Paint

HOW YOU MAKE IT

1. Cut six seatback boards 35" long from deck boards. Orient them vertically and place them in a row on a flat, level work surface. Use spacers to maintain a ½" gap between each board.

2. Cut a lower cross brace 23½" long from a stringer. Screw it across the bottom of the seatback boards, flush with the sides and bottoms, using 2" wood screws.

3. Measure and mark the horizontal center line of the seatback. Cut a 19½"-long upper cross brace from a deck board. Center it side to side, with the bottom edge aligned on the center line. Screw it to the seatback boards with 1½" wood screws.

4. On the front of the seatback, measure and mark points 10" down from the two middle seatback boards, with the points centered side to side. Drive a nail at each point. Use these points for a trammel compass, set at 10". Scribe semicircles from the top of each board, off to the side.

5. Use a jigsaw to cut the boards along the arc cut line.

6. Cut two 33" legs from unnotched stringers (or 2×4s if your stringers are notched). Cut a fascia board and five seat slats 26½" long from deck boards. Screw the fascia across the ends of the legs with 2" wood screws.

7. Line the seat slats up along the legs starting at the fascia board. Maintain a ½" gap between each board. Drill pilot holes and fasten the slats to the legs with finish nails.

8. Fasten the back to the seat legs by sliding the back down between the legs perpendicular to the seat. The top of the seatback's lower brace should be even with the top edge of the legs. Screw the legs to the seatback's lower cross brace with three 3" wood screws on each side.

9. Cut the front legs 20" long from a stringer. Measure and mark a line 15" up from what will be the bottom of each leg. Line these reference lines up with the top of the seat on each side. Tack the legs in place and check with a carpenter's square to ensure they are perfectly perpendicular to the seat. Screw them to the long legs with 3" wood screws.

10. Sit the chair on a flat, level work surface. Use a level to mark a cut line across the bottom of the front and back legs, and a matching line across the top of the front legs. Make the cuts with a circular saw.

11. Cut two wide deck boards 30" long for the arms. Measure and mark 3" in from the side along one end. Mark a line from the mark to the diagonal corner at the other end. Cut the tapers on both arms.

12. Hold the arms on both sides level between the top of the front legs and the sides of the seatback (use a level to check placement). Mark the sides of the seatback for the arm brace position. Cut the arm brace 29½" long from a stringer. Screw it to the back of the seatback, with the top edge aligned with the marks, using 2" wood screws.

13. Screw the arms to the braces and front legs, using 2" wood screws. Putty over the screw heads. Sand the chair all over. Paint as shown on page 53, or finish natural if you prefer.

JIGSAW MAGIC

A jigsaw is an especially useful tool when it comes to custom fabricating a project like the **Adirondack Chair** out of pallet wood. Also called a "saber saw," it can make cutting curves, arcs, and even complex shapes almost as simple as marking the shape. Of course, a jigsaw is ideal in other situations as well. You can use it to make simple, quick crosscuts of thinner members such as deck boards. That means a jigsaw can be a great way of trimming all the deck boards in a pallet along one edge of the center stringer when you're cutting the pallet down to make a project two stringers wide. The tool is also the classic solution for finishing the inside corners of intersecting circular saw cuts, to prevent overcutting. Regardless of what you'll be cutting with the jigsaw, here are a few guidelines to use it to its best advantage.

• **Cut slowly.** This is a good idea not only to accurately follow a curving or complex cut line, but also to keep the blade from bending during any cut, which can lead to beveled cut edges rather than sharp, crisp cut surfaces.

• **Keep the shoe flat on the board.** This will help you accurately follow a cut line. Remember to cut on the outside of the cut line and sand back as necessary.

• **Use a finer blade.** Pallet wood is already rough by nature, so it's best not to make coarse cuts and add to your sanding burden. A blade with at least ten teeth per inch is ideal. You can also help prevent chipping by taping the cut area with painter's tape and drawing the cut line on top of the tape.

BUYING THE RIGHT JIGSAW

If you're going to make your pallet projects as easy as possible to execute, it's wise to buy a jigsaw that will do everything you need it to do. Look for a model with a one-quarter-inch universal tang that holds the blade in place with a set screw. This will allow you to buy any brand of blade. If you plan on using the jigsaw often, you may want to look for one with orbital cutting action, which will position the blade at a more aggressive angle to cut through wood more easily. Opting for a longer blade stroke, such as 1", will also reduce the amount of time it takes to get through a cut. Any saw equipped with blade guides will cut more accurately and with less bending and binding. Lastly, choose a saw with variable speeds, an incredibly handy feature. It's especially useful if you're going to be making some of the tricky cuts in more adventurous pallet projects.

A PALLET DECK

The pallet's natural form lends itself to creating sturdy outdoor ground-level decks. Outdoor pallet surfaces can range from the incredibly simple and rough-looking to much more complex and polished structures that present a handsome backyard surface. It's all about whether you choose the quick-and-easy route, using the pallets unmodified and joined in the way that makes the most sense, or if you are willing to deconstruct the pallets and sand and finish them for an upscale appearance.

In either case, start with the outdoor space. If you plan on using the pallets as they are, the space should ideally be divisible by forty or forty-eight inches. Or, if you're a little flexible on the space you want to use, you can dry lay the pallets without securing them and play with the configuration until you're satisfied with the look. In either case, mark the finished outline with lime or landscaping paint.

It's a simple matter to connect whole pallets one by one, by screwing outside stringers together. (You can add a slightly more finished appearance by attaching deck boards as fascia around the outside of the deck to enclose stringer-end gaps.)

However, you can always deconstruct pallets, partially or completely, to build a more conventional deck structure. That usually means using stringers as joists to form box supports for deck boards. This type of construction requires a fair amount of planning and is best worked out on grid paper first. A deck of this type is also a lot more work. But using deconstructed pallet wood offers you a lot more flexibility in the design of the deck. For instance, you can choose to run the deck boards in one direction, in a herringbone pattern, or even diagonally.

Regardless of whether you're using whole pallets, partially deconstructed units, or loose pallet members, you should take the time to properly prepare the site. Dig down at least three inches and add at least one inch of crushed gravel as a base. That will ensure drainage away from the deck and will level the site. If you want a deck flush with the ground, dig down about five inches and fill with one inch of crushed gravel. You can line the site with landscaping fabric under the gravel to ensure that no growth makes its way up through your pallet deck boards.

COLD FRAME

For avid gardeners, two or three seasons simply aren't enough. They want to extend the growing season and enjoy produce when others are reduced to paying for it at the local supermarket. And who can blame them? Fresh lettuce, herbs, and vegetables in winter? That's pretty enticing, even to people who weren't born with a green thumb. The trick is providing the climate for those plants to grow without incurring the cost, effort, and space for a full-blown greenhouse.

The answer? A cold frame. Not only can a cold frame like the one in this project extend your local growing season, it also affords you the opportunity to grow long-season edibles that might not normally survive the seasons in your zone. The structure may be slightly more limited in space than a greenhouse, but it is also almost free to build and entirely portable. Really, you can think of this structure as poor man's greenhouse—simple to construct, easy to maintain, and incredibly productive.

There is a flip side to those benefits, however. Precise temperature control is very difficult in a cold frame; finicky plants are going to require a lot of attention. You'll have to monitor the thermometer inside the cold frame to ensure the temperature doesn't rise out of control. Surprisingly, even in the depth of winter, the midday heat inside a tight cold frame can rise close to triple digits. The actual size of the unit is another restriction. Tall-growing plants won't be able to mature inside the frame.

However, if you want to increase the depth of the cold frame, you can add a base frame constructed as the one described here. Alternatively, you can dig down inside the cold frame, below your ground level, to accommodate larger or taller plants.

Whatever you grow, keep in mind that you should check the temperature twice a day and provide water as needed. You may need to prop open the lid and allow the cold frame to ventilate and cool down.

TOOLS:

Circular saw or table saw

Measuring tape

Carpenter's pencil

Power drill and bits

Staple gun

Palm sander (optional)

MATERIALS:

1 pallet

2" wood screws

3" wood screws

6-mil clear plastic sheeting

Staples

(3) 2" butt hinges

¼×24" dowel

Sandpaper (optional)

Paint (optional)

HOW YOU MAKE IT

1. Cut four 4 x 20" side-panel boards from deck boards. Cut two 6×20" side-panel boards for the top pieces on each side. Measure and mark these boards with trapezoid cuts, from one corner down to a point 1" above the opposite corner. Cut the shapes out of each board.

2. Cut four corner post stakes, two 13½" long and two 12" long, from stringers. Cut one end of each stake into a 3" point.

3. Lay out three deck boards stacked in a column. Align the longer post stakes with the column's top and outside edges, on both sides of the column. Screw them to boards with 2" wood screws. Repeat the process with the shorter stakes and two deck boards (the top front deck board is a wider 6" board) to construct the front wall.

4. Use two deck boards for the lower side boards, screwing them to the front and back stakes flush with the bottom front and back wallboards.

5. Screw the wide end of the triangular top boards to the back wall stakes. Drill pilot holes down through the top edges of the triangular boards at the front, into the bottom side boards. (The boards may be too thin to do this. If so, you can simply use mending plates on both sides of the board to secure the triangular boards to the base frame.) Screw them together with 2" wood screws.

6. Place the cold frame in its final site and pound the stakes to anchor the frame in the ground.

7. Cut and rip the front and back window frame member 2" wide by 36" long from deck boards. Cut and rip the side frame members 2" wide by 21½" long. Lay the pieces out on a flat, level work surface with the sides overlapping the front and back pieces. Drill pocket holes in the face of the long pieces and screw the frame together with 3" wood screws.

8. Measure and mark the placement of the three hinges equidistant along one long window frame edge. If desired, sand and paint the outside of the cold frame (do not paint or finish the inside of the cold frame). Cut a 6-mil clear plastic window to fit over the window frame and staple it to the frame all around.

9. Screw the butt hinges to the frame over the plastic wraparound. Set the window frame in place atop the cold frame and screw the hinges to the back wall.

10. Drill a shallow ¼" hole in the top front post stakes. Drill a very shallow matching hole in the frame, where it sits over the hole in the post stakes (use the dowel to mark those holes). Use a ¼" dowel to prop open the window as necessary for ventilation and working inside the frame.

COLD FRAME STRATEGIES

There are a number of ways to use a cold frame like the one in this project. Use it for the purpose that makes the most sense given what you're growing in your garden, or build more than one cold frame to use them for different gardening goals.

• **Overwinter plants**. If your garden includes plants such as succulents that are susceptible to dying in cold snaps, you can store the plants in the cold frame for the colder months. Prep tender plants for cold frame storage by cutting back the growth as much as reasonable, crowding them in plastic pots in the cold frame, and then mulching gaps between pots and over the soil level of the plants. If you're trying to keep these plants dormant, you'll want to water very sparsely, and it might be wise to swap the clear plastic sheet for a more opaque white plastic sheet.

• **Start seedlings.** This is a classic use for a cold frame. You can grow seedlings right in the soil where they'll ultimately be placed—something that is especially handy for seedlings that don't like to be transplanted—by simple siting the cold frame over the bed where the plants are meant to be grown. You can also use the cold frame more as a greenhouse by growing seedlings in seed trays. In either case, you'll not only be able to start plants much earlier than you otherwise would, but you'll also be easing their transition through the "hardening off" process, because they'll experience a mild version of the temperature swings they would if planted outside in spring. Of course, if you've started seedlings off in a greenhouse or other area inside under lights, you can use the cold frame as a safe space to harden them off without risking killing them.

• **Growing into the autumn frost.** Cold frames are handy at the other end of the growing season as well. Inevitably, if you grow fall crops, the first hard freeze or cold snap comes too early for some of your harvest. Winter squashes, turnips, kale, and even long-season carrots can all benefit from a kiss of frost (which usually makes them sweeter), but a hard freeze can kill the vegetables. By placing a cold frame over these plants, you can let them mature at their pace despite the weather.

DOGHOUSE

This doghouse is a slightly different design than the traditional puppy shelter. It includes a shed roof and enough space inside for even a large dog. By not completely enclosing the spaces between the boards of the walls and ceiling, air and sunlight can penetrate. Those, in turn, keep the inside of the doghouse from getting funky and help stop ticks and fleas from colonizing. There is also a shallow porch in front of the house, where you can set a water bowl or even a food bowl if your pooch decides to spend most of his time outdoors.

However, if you want to make the house weatherproof, you can cover the gaps between the boards on the roof and walls with ripped-down deconstructed deck boards. You can also add solid foam insulation panels on the inside of the walls and roof to winterize Fido's getaway. You can modify it in other ways if you're feeling ambitious. Cut a window on one or both sides, or add a mattress inside for maximum comfort and even a solar-powered light fixture on top so that you can see how your dog is doing at night.

WHAT YOU'LL NEED

Time: **2 hours** | Difficulty: **Hard**

TOOLS:

Pry bar or hammer

Shovel

Level

Measuring tape

Carpenter's pencil

Carpenter's square

Power drill and bits

Circular saw

Paintbrush (optional)

MATERIALS:

3 pallets

Pea gravel (optional)

4" wood screws

3" wood screws

1 ½" wood screws

2" wood screws

Roofing paper (optional)

Shingles (optional)

Paint or finish (optional)

HOW YOU MAKE IT

1. Strip the bottom deck boards from a pallet. Dig out and level a 42×50" area in the yard for the doghouse, and add a 1" layer of pea gravel. (The doghouse can also be placed on a patio or other solid surface.) Set the foundation pallet in place and check for level both ways.

2. Remove three top and bottom deck boards at one end of two pallets. Measure and mark 38" from one end of an edge stringer, 36" on the center stringer, and 34" on the other edge stringer. Cut the stringers for both pallets along the marks with a jigsaw.

3. Stand one pallet on the uncut stringer ends, flush to the outside edge and back of the foundation. (The front will be recessed from the front of the foundation.) Check the wall for plumb with a carpenter's square and brace it in place. Toe-screw 4" wood screws down through the wall's stringers, into the foundation stringer. Repeat the process with the opposite wall.

4. Strip the bottom deck boards off a pallet for the roof. Use a helper to set the pallet, deck board side up, on top of the walls. (The roof pallet should be oriented in the same direction as the foundation.) Adjust the roof so that the back projects about ¾" out from the back edge of the walls.

5. Toe-screw the roof stringers on both sides to the wall stringers on both sides. Remove the wall braces.

6. Screw deck boards as fascia across the stringer ends on both ends of the roof, with 3" wood screws. Cut four side fascia boards 24¾" long from deck boards. Screw two to each side, overlapping the edges of the front and back fascia boards and butted at the center.

2

3

4

7. Cut an upper nailer 33" long and a soleplate 18" long from stringers. Screw the nailer between the walls at the top of the front stringers (the longest stringers). Screw the soleplate to the foundation butted to the left wall stringer, flush with the front edge of the stringer.

8. Cut a 33" soleplate from a stringer and screw it face-down between the walls, flush with the back of the walls and foundation.

9. Cut twelve back wallboards 36¾" long from deck boards. Install a nailer at the top of the wall as you did in the front of the doghouse. Starting from the outside edge of one wall stringer, screw the back wallboards in place. They should be flush on the bottom with the bottom of the foundation's deck boards. The top of the wallboards will run behind the rear roof fascia board and will be screwed to the nailer with 1½" wood screws. The final back wallboard will need to be ripped down to approximately 1½". Measure and adjust to fit the final spacing.

10. Cut six front wallboards 41½" long from deck boards. Screw them in place between the upper nailer and soleplate, starting in front of the left wall's stringer, using 2" wood screws.

11. Measure and mark deck boards to cover the triangular gaps at the top of both walls. Screw the boards in place. Measure any significant gaps in the walls and roof of the doghouse and rip deck boards to fit the gaps as necessary. You can also cover the roof with roofing felt stapled to the deck boards, or other weatherproof covering, to make the doghouse entirely weatherproof.

12. Paint or finish as desired, and add a dog bed to make the house more comfortable for your pet.

WORKBENCH

Who doesn't need a sturdy workbench?

Indoors or out, a workbench is an incredibly handy structure, as a place to park tools and supplies and a rugged surface for crafting projects small and large. When it comes to simple, durable, tough, and portable workbenches, you'll be hard-pressed to top the one in this project.

It's basically just three pallets combined in a way that ensures a durable work surface, one on which you won't be afraid to chop, drill, cut, or splash paint. Leave it out in the yard during a rainstorm? No worries. It's pallet wood after all. It will take all that the elements can throw at it and be ready for you when you start your next project.

It's also a compact, portable table. All you need is a helper to move it anywhere you want to work. Once you get it there, you'll find that the workbench supports a surprising amount of weight. Pile a chop saw, portable grinder, or other power tool right on top without worrying about the table getting wobbly.

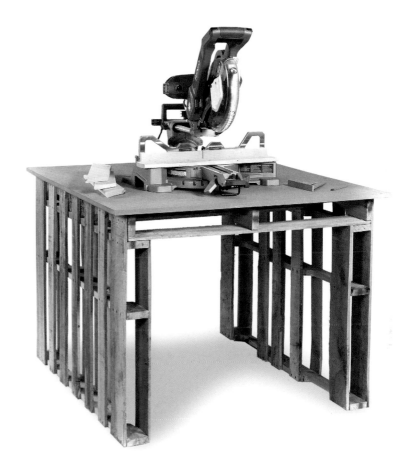

WHAT YOU'LL NEED

Time: **30 minutes** | Difficulty: **Easy**

TOOLS:

Measuring tape
Carpenter's pencil

Circular saw
Power drill and bits
Carpenter's square
Hammer

MATERIALS:

3 pallets
3" wood screws
4" wood screws
Brads

HOW YOU MAKE IT

1. Modify two pallets for the workbench legs. Cut the top deck boards 35¼" long. Cut the bottom deck boards 31" long (or the length of the top deck boards minus the thickness of the pallets you're using, including top and bottom deck boards—the pallets used here were 4¼" thick).

2. Remove the board remnants from both sides of the stringer that was removed from each leg when you made the board cuts. Screw it in place between the legs' top and bottom deck boards, with the top face flush with the top of the shorter boards on the legs.

3. Stand the legs in place, parallel to each other and with the cut sides up (you can brace them by tacking a waste deck board edge to edge across the legs).

4. Nest the edges of a full pallet, bottom side down, into the cutouts at the top of the two legs.

5. Use a carpenter's square to check that the legs are plumb to the top. Screw the legs' outside deck boards to the top's stringers on both sides, using 3" wood screws.

6. Drive 4" wood screws up through the legs' top stringers into the top surface's stringers on both sides.

7. Add a top working surface to the workbench, such as a sheet of ¾" plywood (used here) or medium-density fiberboard. Nail it down with brads. You can cut it to match the dimensions of the table exactly, or allow for 2 to 3" of overhang, as with this table.

SANDBOX

If you want to combat the hypnotic draw of TV and other electronic devices for your youngsters, turn to the simplest of play structures—an old-fashioned sandbox.

The allure of a sandbox is based in imagination. Add a toy car and your kids can place themselves in a road rally through the Sahara. A pail and plastic shovel is all they need to craft an enviable medieval castle to defend from imaginary marauders.

What's even better, the structure is easy to construct. Start building it on a Saturday morning and your kids will be playing in it by noon.

Don't be tempted to shortcut any of the project. The weed-blocking landscape fabric will keep the sandbox from becoming a garden bed, and the cover is a necessity to keep neighborhood pets and area wildlife from making the box their own.

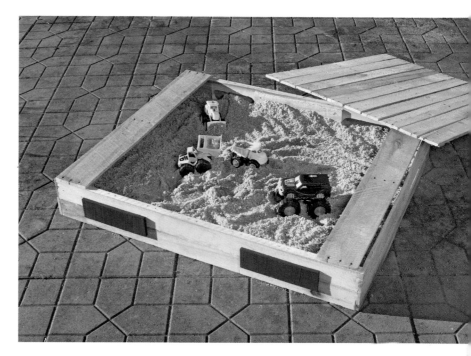

WHAT YOU'LL NEED

Time: **30 minutes** | Difficulty: **Easy**

TOOLS:
Pry bar or hammer
Power drill and bits
Measuring tape
Circular saw
Staple gun

MATERIALS:
2 pallets
3" wood screws
1 ½" wood screws
1 ⅜" brads
2" wood screws
Landscape fabric
Sterilized beach sand

HOW YOU MAKE IT

1. Deconstruct a pallet, and use two of the stringers and two deck boards to construct a basic 40 x 49½" frame by screwing the deck boards to the ends of the stringers with 3" wood screws. Check the corners for square by measuring the diagonals (they should match exactly). Set it in place with the stringer notches facing up.

2. Strip a second pallet of all its bottom boards, its center stringer, and all but the end boards on top—leave one board if the end boards are 1 x 6" and two if they are 1 x 4". Sit the pallet on top of the sandbox frame with the stringer notches facing down, so that the top and bottom stringers are perfectly flush and the notches form an oval opening in the side of the sandbox.

3. Use scrap pieces of 1 x 6" or 1 x 4" as braces to fasten the two pallets together. Screw the braces in place on both sides. Screw a deck board across each end of the top frame pallet.

4. Cut four plates 12" long from deck boards to cover the holes created by the stringer notches on each side. Screw them over the holes with 1½" wood screws.

5. Construct the sandbox cover by lining up nine deck boards spaced ½" apart. Measure them side to side, and then measure from the inside of one sandbox top board to the other. The cover must fit inside this space. Adjust as necessary.

6. Center two 32" braces cut from stringers side to side across the cover boards (positioned 3" in from top and bottom). Tack the braces to the boards using a hammer and 1⅜" brads (or use a hammer

and predrill the holes if you prefer), flip the cover, and screw each board to both braces with 2" wood screws.

7. Place the sandbox in its final location. Line the bottom with landscaping fabric and staple the fabric to the interior sides of the box. Paint the faceplates on each side as a decorative element. Fill the sandbox with natural sterilized beach sand meant for playground use.

Alternative: If you want to add comfort to the sandbox or just make it a little fancier, screw 14" supports cut from stringers on each end of the sandbox in back of the bench deck boards, and screw deck boards to the supports to form a back for the bench seats at each end.

SANDBOX SAFETY PRACTICES

As fun as they can be, sandboxes can also represent a potential health hazard if they are not properly maintained. Start with the sand.

• Use only natural, cleaned river or beach sand in the sandbox. Avoid any bagged or loose product that contains crushed limestone, marble, silica (quartz), or other filler. Dust from these products has been linked to respiratory illnesses.

• If you find that insects are infiltrating the sandbox, consider covering the underside of the cover and bench seats with landscape fabric or plastic sheeting. You can also create a framed cover from plastic sheeting and a frame of deck boards, or use the much simpler solution of draping a tarp over the sandbox

when it's not in use. Secure the edges with rocks or other weights.

• If the sand gets wet, rake it as it dries, to ensure the sand on the bottom of the box doesn't stay wet.

• Rake through the sand regularly to remove any debris that might have found its way into the sandbox.

QUICK 3

One of the great features of pallets is that they can be stacked, butted together, and arranged like rough-hewn building blocks in an incredible diversity of configurations. The three projects here are simple garden structures that require little in the way of engineering, expertise, or exacting precision. They're crude, but useful. They're also exceptionally adaptable. You can cut down the **Vertical Planter**, for instance, to fit the available space on a wall or fence. Double up pallets for the **Pallet Fencing** to create a much thicker, more substantial barrier where one is needed. No matter how you play with the designs of these, the basic function of each structure doesn't vary. Neither does the fact that they are all extremely practical. A vertical planter allows you to grow a kitchen herb garden in a limited amount of space—or create a cascading living wall with sprawling foliage plants. A fence can protect an edible garden from wildlife or even pets who want their share of the bounty. And a compost bin doesn't need to be pretty or complicated to produce "black gold" for your soil and your garden plants. There's no denying that these three are not inherently the most beautiful things you'll make with pallets. That's not the point. The real sell is their utility and the fact that each of these only takes a few minutes of your time and some basic tools to put together. And yet, they're sure to last as long—or longer—than any store-bought alternatives.

1. HANDY VERTICAL PLANTER

Garden space limited? Don't worry—garden up rather than out by planting your own customized vertical planter. You'll use the top deck boards for mounting the planter to the surface where it will receive the most light. The planter couldn't be easier to construct. Remove bottom deck boards from a pallet, leaving only the ends and middle boards. Fold landscape fabric into pockets to fit the cavities behind the remaining boards, and dry fit them. Once you're happy with the fit, use a staple gun to staple the fabric pockets into place between the top and bottom deck boards. Mount the planter on a wood fence or wood siding with screws, or attach it to a cyclone fence by drilling holes through the boards and wiring the planter to the fence. In either case, use more fasteners than you think necessary, because the weight of wet soil and mature plants can easily more than double the dry weight of the planter. If you're looking for an easier solution, just lean the pallet planter up against a vertical surface; it isn't likely to budge once you have planted it. The more important consideration is that the sun exposure in the location you've chosen is adequate for the plants you've selected. Ideally, you'll want six to eight hours of direct sun for most edible plants; shade-loving plants will tolerate considerably less sun. Plant the planter with your favorite herbs, shallow-rooted vegetables, or bushy flowers, but keep in mind the mature spacing. Because the plants are growing in the best possible soil, with optimal watering, they'll definitely fill out to larger than their normal mature sizes.

2. PALLET FENCING

Because of the limited dimensions of the average pallet, the deconstructed wood members are usually only appropriate for half-height fences. In that sense, the wood can be ideal for a small picket fence or similar barrier. However, when all you need is a functional, rustic-looking border, look no

further than the closest pile of pallets. For durable fence sections, remove two courses of boards at one end of the pallet and use the exposed stringer ends as posts to secure the pallet in the ground. Screw additional fence sections, stringer face to stringer face, to create a length of fence, and screw perpendicular pallets together at fence corners. Leave both the top and bottom boards on each pallet for a sturdier fence, or remove all the bottom boards and position the pallets with the top boards facing out to create a more traditional look. Sandwich two pallets together for an incredibly stable base on which you can add a top pallet to make a taller fence.

3. COMPOST BIN

A compost bin is a must-have for a productive garden and an environmentally responsible household. The structure lets you turn much of your kitchen waste into gardening black gold. Simply set three pallets on edge with the stringer faces lying on the ground, and screw the pallets together at the corners to create a U shape. Place the bin in a discreet corner of the garden and add kitchen and yard waste on a regular basis. Water your compost pile regularly, but don't allow it to become soaked. Never put animal waste, fats, meats or other proteins, or baked goods into the pile. Turn the compost at least once a week, and in a couple of months, you'll have a wonderful soil amendment.

HAMMOCK CHAIR

Nothing screams "lazy summer day" quite like a hammock. Unfortunately, traditional fabric hammocks tend to ruin that first impression. They are prone to staying wet for a long time after the morning dew or a rainstorm, and the outdoor exposure can lead to dirt buildup, mold, and mildew. Using a hammock that hasn't been cleaned in a while can seem a lot like jumping into an old gym sock for an afternoon nap.

A sling chair like the one in this project is a way to enjoy the relaxing promise of a hammock without the gross downsides. This unique construction creates a chair that conforms to your body, creating an incredibly relaxing sitting position. But the tight weave of the nylon rope ensures the integrity of the chair over time and frequent use. The rope itself is a superior choice to metal chain or standard rope, either of which will irritate the skin over time and are uncomfortable in any case. Today's nylon rope is soft and accommodating.

The design is both flexible and strong, even under the weight of a large person. The key is to ensure the hanging hardware is every bit as strong. Although you can use thick rope to hang the chair—an option that looks much nicer than metal links—zinc-coated chain is a sturdier alternative that will head off any chance of failure. Of course, you'll also need to hang the chair from a solid support, such as porch joists. When in doubt, err on the side of caution.

WHAT YOU'LL NEED

Time: **1 hour** | Difficulty: **Easy**

TOOLS:

Circular saw

Router and ⅛ roundover bit

Paintbrush (optional)

Palm sander

Power drill and bits

Scissors or utility knife

Lighter

MATERIALS:

1 pallet

80- and 100-grit sandpaper

½" wood dowel

Paint or finish (optional)

(4) ⁵/₁₆"×3-¼" eye bolts with machine threads, lock nuts, and fender washers

40' length of ⅜" nylon SB rope or paracord

Duct tape

4 quick links

HOW YOU MAKE IT

1. Cut fifteen seat slats 20" long from deck boards. Sand the slats smooth all over with 100-grit, then 80-grit sandpaper.

2. Drill ⅝" holes at the edges of one board, 1" in from the top and sides, and 1" in from the bottom and sides. Drill matching holes 2" in from each of these holes. Use this seat slat as a template to mark the other slats for drilling.

3. Use a dowel wrapped with sandpaper taped into place to clean up the holes and smooth any sharp edges. Round out the holes with a router equipped with a ⅛" roundover bit. If you're sealing or finishing the chair, do that now and allow the boards to dry completely before assembly.

4. Drill mounting holes for the eye bolts between the sets of holes on the topmost seat slat and second to last slat in the chair.

5. Cut a 40' piece of nylon rope. Tie one end into a thick, tight knot. Wrap the opposite end in duct tape. Starting at what will be the top seat slat, run the unknotted end down through the top outside hole and then up through the bottom hole. Run it into the second slat's top hole, and repeat the process to the last seat slat in the chair.

6. At the last slat, bring the rope up through the bottom hole and over to the opposite bottom hole, and run the rope back up to the top in the same way. At the top, run the rope over to the opposite inside top hole, and thread the rope through the opposite set of slat holes in the same way.

7. At the final hole, pull the rope to ensure the chair structure is tight from the knotted end forward, then tie a slip knot to secure the rope. Melt it slightly with a lighter.

8. Attach the eye bolts at the top and bottom of the chair with a lock nut for each and fender washers on each side. Hang the chair from the eye bolts with quick links (the chair can be suspended from tree branches or from eye hooks in the joists of a porch). Try out different heights to change the angle of the seat, as desired.

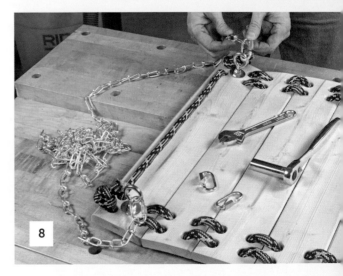

3 STORAGE

Interior designers and homeowners alike know for a fact that you can never have too much storage. And though you usually can't throw together a new walk-in closet, there are a bevy of incredibly useful storage accessories that you can make for little or no money, and that will help you keep everything in its place.

The projects in this chapter provide specific storage to deal with common clutter in the house. There's something here for just about every room—from the kitchen to the clothes closet to a child's bedroom. And these are just the beginning; many of these creations will no doubt spur you own ideas for innovative storage units suited specifically to you and your family.

COAT RACK AND SHELF

There's just no denying that a wall-mounted coat rack can be exceptionally handy, but it's also one of those small additions to the home that homeowners never seem to get around to buying.

Why spend the money? A coat rack, like the one shown here, is an easy thing to build. You won't even need a full pallet, and you most likely have all the tools you'll need to put yours together. Start on Saturday morning and chances are you'll have it finished and up on the wall before the rest of the family gets home from the soccer or baseball game.

This particular rack's design is adaptable. You can resize the rack to suit your available wall space or to add decorative elements that match your home's look. The finish you choose and the hooks you include will both set the tone of the rack and determine whether it becomes an entryway focal point or blends almost invisibly with the room. You can choose from antique options that are decorative flourishes or clean chrome hooks for a more contemporary look.

The more important decision you'll have to make is the number of hooks. Make sure that you have more hooks than you need. If a coat doesn't have a place to go, it inevitably winds up draped over the back of a chair or, worse, lying on the floor somewhere. That not only makes for a clutter eyesore, it also shortens the lifespan of foul-weather gear.

WHAT YOU'LL NEED

TOOLS:

Pry bar

Circular saw

Speed square

Power drill and bits

Pocket hole jig

Orbital sander

Stud finder

Paintbrush (optional)

MATERIALS:

1 pallet

3" wood screws

2 ½" pocket hole screws

100-grit sandpaper

Coat hooks and mounting screws

1 quart gloss white paint (optional)

HOW YOU MAKE IT

1. Remove the bottom deck boards from a pallet, and cut the stringers 16½" from one end, or so that there are three top deck boards remaining attached to the stringer section.

2. Use a speed square to mark the cut end of the stringers for a 45° cut. Cut the miters with a circular saw.

3. Use 3" wood screws to fasten a deck board across the uncut ends of the stringers.

4. Cut two shelves 21¾" long from a deck board. Use a pocket hole jig to drill pocket holes in each end. Position the shelves 3½" up from the bottom of the miters, and screw them in place with 2½" pocket hole screws.

5. Sand the unit all over and paint as desired. Screw two coat hooks onto the bottom deck board on each side of the central stringer.

6. Use a stud finder to locate the wall studs and screw the rack to the wall at the desired location with 3" wood screws. Putty over the screws, sand, and touch up the paint as necessary.

THE COAT RACK RULES

For such a simple thing, placing a coat rack thoughtfully makes all the difference between whether it is convenient and intuitive to use or a bother.

• **Height.** The Americans with Disabilities Act calls for an accessible coat rack to be placed no more than forty-eight inches from the floor. This is also an excellent rule of thumb for a house with children in it. If kids can't reach the coat rack, chances are their coats are going to wind up on a chair or on the floor. Of course, you need to accommodate all the occupants of the house, so it may make the most sense to include two coat racks—one high and one low.

• **Support.** The coat rack is screwed into studs, which is an ideal practice. If you use anchors because your coat rack placement doesn't fall neatly on studs, make sure the anchors are rated for the appropriate weight. It isn't just a matter of how much the coat rack weighs; you have to take into account the rack plus the weight of outer gear that may be wet.

• **Coat rack partners.** Because outer gear can often be both wet and dirty, it's always wise to include some sort of absorbent mat under a coat rack. There are many types to choose from, including the informal handsome appearance of a coir mat or a miniature throw rug. The best mats, though, are washable and dry quickly. Along with the mat, a small bench or place to sit is a natural companion—after taking off their coats, visitors or family members will probably need to take off boots or shoes to avoid tracking mud or water into the house. Which is why most entryway benches are coupled with a shoe rack of one sort or another (you can find a sturdy, durable option on page 94).

• **Compatible storage.** A small, shallow basket for gloves, keys, or cell phones or a larger wooden bin for foul-weather footwear are both optimal complements to a coat rack— especially one like the rack in this project, featuring an integral shelf. The key to beating entryway clutter is to ensure there is a place for anything that comes in through the door.

WINE AND LIQUOR BOTTLE RACK

In this age of the wine box, if you're buying and storing wine bottles, you might as well show them off. And what better way to do that then to build a wonderfully rustic rack that juxtaposes the sleek, sophisticated look of wine bottles (or the subtle colorations of liquor bottles) against the earthy appeal of pallet wood.

It's a simple rack to build; the hardest part is making the curving cut in the three stringers of the pallet, but that's also a chance for even more creativity. You can create a simple curving pattern as with this rack, create one more involved, or even settle on a more geometric approach for a modern look. Of course, if you're not comfortable with a jigsaw, you can always just miter the stringers from the front edge of the rail back to the mounting boards.

You can also vary the look of the rack. Although we've distressed and stained the rack shown here (to capture the charm of a vineyard barrel), you can certainly finish it natural for a more understated approach. If you're a little crafty, you can even stencil a fun saying or other words on the front of the rack, or paint the whole thing in an eye-catching color scheme. Just be done by cocktail hour!

WHAT YOU'LL NEED

Time: **20 minutes** | Difficulty: **Easy**

TOOLS:

Circular saw
Measuring tape
Pry bar
Carpenter's pencil
Jigsaw
Palm sander

Power drill and bits
Level
Paintbrush
Stud finder

MATERIALS:

1 pallet

Grid paper
Cardboard
80-grit sandpaper
3" wood screws
Bolt and nut
10" length of ³/₈" chain
Walnut stain
Wood putty

HOW YOU MAKE IT

1. Use a circular saw to cut the stringers of a pallet 13" from one end, or to the inside edge of the third top deck board from the end.

2. Remove all but the end bottom deck board (the top deck boards will serve as the back of the wine rack). Work out a curved pattern for the stringer faces on a piece of grid paper. Transfer the design to a piece of cardboard and cut it out to create a template.

3. Use the template to trace the cutting lines on the face of each stringer. Cut along the lines with a jigsaw, and sand the surfaces after you're done.

4. Screw a deck board to the uncut ends of the stringers, using 3" wood screws. Secure a bolt and nut at the end of a small length of chain and whip the chain, alternating ends, against the surface of the wood, focusing on the stringers. Don't hit the wood so hard that you break any member—the goal is to convincingly distress the surface.

5. Stain the wood with a walnut stain as used here, or similar stain, to enhance the distressed appearance.

6. Once the stain has dried, use a stud finder to locate and mark the studs on the wall to which the rack will be mounted. Use a helper to hold the rack up to the desired height, and check for level.

7. Drill and countersink mounting holes for 3" wood screws, and screw the rack to the wall, checking level again before tightening the screws. Dab wood putty over the screw heads and, when dry, sand and dab with stain.

DON'T FORGET THE WINE GLASSES

If your kitchen is space challenged, you may want the wine rack in this project to work a little bit harder. Obviously, the rack can be expanded, or you can craft several of them, to use for liquor bottles, olive oil and vinegars, or any bottled ingredient. But with a slight modification to this project plan, you can also store wine glasses and other stemware with the rack.

Start by cutting two two-inch-wide pieces from the end of a stringer. Line the pieces up as extensions on the bottom of the wine rack's stringers (under the board that serves as the floor for the wine bottles). Screw these extenders to the board and up into the stringer ends.

Cut slots spaced four inches apart in a deck board. The slots should be cut from one edge, into the face of the board, stopping about one inch from the opposite edge. They should be parallel with the ends of the board, and each slot should each be three-quarters to one inch wide. The slots can be cut with multiple passes from a table saw or a router.

To complete the glass hanger, screw the board to the bottom of the blocks, with the slot openings facing the front of the wine rack. Now you can simply slide wine glass stems into the slots so that the glasses hang down below the wine. As a bonus, the glasses couldn't look cooler!

SMALL WALL-MOUNTED SHELF

Sometimes smaller is better. If all you need is a small display shelf for curios, collections, small pictures, or knickknacks, a full-size bookshelf would not only be overkill, it would be wasted space.

That's where this small display shelf comes in. It's compact enough that it won't get in the way of foot traffic, even in a hall or other confined quarters. It's simple enough to build and so basic in design that you may be able to construct it with leftovers from other pallet projects. Fortunately, though, it's sturdy enough to display even heavy items.

The shelf shown here has been finished natural, which allows whatever's stored on the shelves to grab all the attention. But you could just as easily paint it to suit your home's interior, and even accent it with stencils or a little free-hand brushwork to show your artistic side.

WHAT YOU'LL NEED

Time: **15 minutes** | Difficulty: **Easy**

TOOLS:

Circular saw
Pry bar or hammer
Measuring tape
Power drill and bits

Stud finder
Sanding block

MATERIALS:

1 pallet

3" wood screws
2" casing nails
Wood putty
Sandpaper
Polyurethane sealer

HOW YOU MAKE IT

1. Use a circular saw to cut the top deck boards of a pallet along one edge of the central stringer. Cut the remaining two-stringer section 21" long.

2. Remove all the top deck boards on the stringer section. Remove the bottom deck boards, leaving the end board and the one on the other side of the notch.

3. Cut two of the removed deck boards 20¾" long. Screw each onto one end of the stringers with 3" wood screws (the boards should be flush with the stringers).

4. Cut a shelf 17¾" long from a deck board. Measure and mark 12" up from one end of the frame. Hold the shelf in position and drill pilot holes from outside into the shelf edges. Drill pilot holes and nail the shelf in place with 2" casing nails. (If the deck boards you've reclaimed are too thin for this, you can mount the shelf with metal L brackets—just make sure the shelf is level.)

5. Use a stud finder to locate the studs where you want to hang the shelf. Drill mounting holes through the back boards. Putty all the screw heads, let dry, and sand the shelf. Finish it natural with a polyurethane sealer. Screw the shelf to the studs with 3" wood screws.

PALLETS AS ART

Pallets are so practical and functional—as are most of the projects you make from them—that it is often surprising to discover how wonderful they can be for pure arts-and-crafts projects. Free pallets give you the chance to creatively express yourself without risking much in the way of time or money. They also allow you to spruce up your home with personal artworks that put your own signature on your décor. And last but not least, arts projects are exceptional uses for the odds and ends leftover from other pallet projects—scraps that might otherwise just become fire starters. The list here represents just a few of the decorative and artistic uses for pallets and pallet wood. Let your imagination run wild and you'll surely find many, many more.

• **Signs.** If you think about it, a pallet set on its side so that the deck boards run horizontally bears more than a passing resemblance to lined paper. That's why unmodified pallets make such good surfaces for displaying words. Use stencils or write freehand to re-create lines of poems on the deck boards, capture a particularly poignant quote, or just point the way to your home's man cave. No matter what words you're featuring, there are all kinds of ways to make them artsy. Paint the boards underneath in a contrasting, or even a complementary, color from the letters for a dynamic look that will really punch up whatever it is you write. Use cursive letters or other unusual fonts for added visual interest. You can even paint the letters in different colors to really give the sign an unusual appearance.

• **Standalone artworks.** The deck boards of a pallet can be a canvas on which to draw, paint, or screen an image. The gaps between boards make for eye-catching visual interruptions in any picture. You can also fill in the gaps with ripped-down boards to create a solid surface for just about any picture or image you can imagine. The downside is that the stringers will make your artwork very heavy and awkward to mount. That's why a lot of budding artists deconstruct the pallet and make a custom canvas by sawing deck boards to a preferred length and using cleats on the back to join the boards in a flat, paintable surface.

• **Shapes.** A common way crafters use pallet wood is to cleat deck boards together in a tight, flat surface; trace a shape on top; and then use a jigsaw to cut out the shape. It's a great way to make a map shape, something simple like a star, or even a more abstract shape. Paint the shape in whatever color you desire to create an interesting piece of mountable wall art.

This interesting interpretation of the American flag, through the lens of Texas, uses the negative space between deck boards in a natural way.

HANGING POT RACK

If you've ever clanked your way through pots or pans in a drawer looking for just the right sauté pan, you'll know that these essential cookware items are some of the most difficult kitchen tools to store. That doesn't have to be the case though; there's plenty of room overhead.

Hanging a pot rack from your ceiling is not only a way to organize pots and pans in an at-a-glance fashion; it also makes some of the most-used equipment in the kitchen much more conveniently accessible. All that, and it frees up lots of drawer space for your other kitchen necessities.

It's also a great look that pretty much advertises "an avid cook works here." The rack in this project is finished with a natural appearance common to most wooden pot racks, because the look of the wood so perfectly complements the rugged nature of steel and cast-iron cookware. That said, you can certainly paint the rack if you prefer. Just be aware that dirt, dust, and smoke all float up in the kitchen—maybe more so than you realize. If you opt for a glossy white finish, or other bright color, you'll have to plan on regular cleanings.

This is a simple rack to build and even simpler to adapt. It may be that you have a smaller kitchen, or just an oddly shaped room. That's okay; you can make this design narrower, shorter, or just plain smaller, and it will be still be super useful. In any case, take your time in deciding on a height to hang the rack; it should be at the ideal height for the person who cooks most in the kitchen. If you're worried about support, you can reinforce the hanging connection by installing the cleats described in the **Porch Swing** project on page 40 and using longer, thicker ceiling screw eyes.

HANGING OUT

Where and how you hang your pot rack is a matter of heading off any potential problems while making the rack as convenient as possible for the cooks who use the kitchen most. Here are some guidelines for trouble-free pot hanging:

• Avoid the temptation to hang the pot rack near a window. There will be some degree of swing in any hanging pot rack as you remove and replace cookware, and a swinging cast iron pan can easily smash a window.

• Although we've specified that the rack should be mounted low enough for the shortest cook in the kitchen to reach, that only holds true if the rack has been mounted over a surface such as a counter. If the rack hangs over open floor space, you'll want to adjust it so that the bottoms of the pans are high enough for the tallest user of the kitchen to pass under them. The shorter cook can use a folding step stool to reach the cookware.

• Whenever possible, hang the rack over a kitchen island, a stove, or some other surface, because a falling pot or pan could hurt anyone standing under the rack and could easily damage a tile or laminate kitchen floor.

HOW YOU MAKE IT

1. Remove the bottom deck boards from a pallet and cut the top boards to one edge of the center stringer, so that the rack is two stringers wide. Cut the stringers 24¾" from one end. Depending on board placement, this may involve removing a board or ripping it to suit. You may also want to cut the stringers from each end to center the notches, if any.

2. Use a speed square to mark a 45° miter on the ends of the stringers, narrowing the stringers toward the open side. Make the cuts with a circular saw.

3. Cut a center brace 21¾" long, from the third waste stringer. Place the brace face down between the two rack stringers, centered along their length. Screw the stringers to the brace ends with 3" wood screws.

4. Sand or distress the rack as desired, and paint or finish it. (The rack shown here was left natural.)

5. Screw 4" ceiling hooks 14" to 16" apart and centered along the top edge of each stringer. Screw 3" ceiling hooks to the bottom faces of the deck boards (now the underside of the pot rack). Position one hook at each end of each deck board, screwing it up into a stringer. Center a hook along the length of center brace. If your deck boards are ¾" or thicker, you can add more screw hooks.

6. Use a stud finder to mark ceiling joist locations. Screw 4" ceiling hooks into the ceiling joists and use lengths of ²⁄₀ chain to hang the rack from the ceiling.

Alternative: If hanging the rack from a wall, use a stud finder to mark stud location. Screw one side of the rack to the wall with 3" wood screws. Screw 4" ceiling hooks to the same studs at the top of the wall, and run the chain between the wall hooks and the outside stringer hooks.

3

5

6

POT-HANGING OPTIONS & ALTERNATIVES

The project here is amazingly adaptable to your own circumstances and the available space and configuration in your kitchen. Be creative when considering how you might want to mount or modify this pot hanger.

• **It's not just for pots and pans!** Use the hooks in the face of the deck boards—or anywhere, for that matter—to support utensils. Having the right spatula nearby and ready for use can be indispensable, and, arguably, most cooks use utensils even more than they use their cookware. Of course, if you really want to vary the look or get the most out of your pot hanger, add a row of smaller hooks for coffee mugs or beer steins.

• **Go small.** Have a galley kitchen or similar small space? You can modify the pot hanger in this project to suit. You might even want to simply mount a single stringer on edge to your ceiling joists with countersunk six-inch lag screws, and then line the stringer bottom edge with hooks. For a longer hanger, butt two stringers together.

• **Go wall.** Although we've included a half-wall-mounted option in the instructions for this project, you can take the idea one step further.

In the simplest sense, you can screw the pot hanger as it is (without the ceiling hooks on top) directly to wall studs and then hang pots and pans from the hooks that project out horizontally. You can also deconstruct a pallet and form you own custom hanger from different pieces, secured to the wall. This is a way to put blank wall space to good use and tailor the look and size of the rack to exactly suit the pots and pans you need to hang.

Rounded ends add flair to a wall-mounted pot hanger made from deconstructed pallet boards. The dark stain helps hide flaws and imperfections, and makes the perfect foil for copper pans.

LARGE BOOKSHELF

Bookshelves are some of the most versatile and just plain handiest pieces of storage furniture in any house. The bookshelf in this project is sized specifically to accommodate books, but it is ideal for storing many objects. Dress it up with paint and perhaps some subtle stenciling, and it can be a wonderful dining room display cabinet for your favorite glassware. Paint different sections in contrasting primary colors and it will fit right in to your toddler's bedroom as a vibrant home for toys or your child's favorite illustrated books. Or go with a more understated stain or natural finish and use the bookshelf in your home office to keep office supplies in order and within arm's reach.

No matter what you use it for, this bookshelf will bring a handsome look to any room. The split sides are a slightly craftsman-style touch, forming a stable base on which the bookshelf stands. The fascia boards that front the shelves hide the shelf brackets and give the unit a lovely finished look. For ease of fabrication, and to create a visual back for the bookshelves, the deck boards have been left attached to the stringer pair that forms the back legs of the bookshelf. The deck boards could be removed with the help of a reciprocating saw to give the bookshelves a more conventional appearance—but think twice about doing that. The deck boards add a lot of stability and will keep the bookshelves square over time. They can also be ideal for securing the bookshelf to a wall for added stability.

One of the most wonderful things about this bookshelf is that—like most pieces of pallet furniture—it's very adaptable. Have a bigger library of books? Make a wider bookshelf by using a full pallet of three stringers (don't remove the central stringer—it will keep the shelves from sagging under the load of heavy books). Want to go more vertical? Stack a second pallet bookshelf unit on top (see **Safe Stacking** opposite). Another excellent trait of this unit is that it is entirely portable, and you'll find it easy to move wherever you need it.

You can also switch up the design, as you prefer. Rip and cut a deck board to fill in the vertical gap on each side if you prefer a "closed" bookshelf. Although the bookshelf in this project has been painted yellow, it would look handsome painted white or a neutral color. If you're using it in a more colorful or funky setting, you can paint it with different colors for the legs and the shelves, or one bright color with stenciled designs down the legs. Ultimately, the choice is to finish it to blend in or stand out, but keep in mind that rows of books are a wonderful visual that stands out all on their own.

SAFE STACKING

The beauty of a bookshelf like the one in this project is that it can be stacked to create a taller unit with double the capacity. But any time you stack individual bookshelf units, it's important to ensure the structure is entirely safe. You don't want to find out it's unstable after you have filled it with heavy books.

Given the variable thicknesses of the deck boards from different pallets, it's wise to permanently fix a stacked unit to the lower bookshelf with horizontal cleats screwed across the joint where the top rests on the bottom. You can attach the cleats on the inside or outside, but they will actually look better on the outside of the bookshelves and will not take up real estate that could be used by books.

You should also secure stacked bookshelves to the wall. There are many ways to do this; you'll find solutions such as security straps at hardware stores and home centers, or you can simply screw the bookshelves to the wall by driving screws through the back deck boards and into wall studs.

In any case, avoid stacking shelves in areas of heavy traffic flow, where people will often bump the bookcases.

Also follow common-sense rules for how you place books on the shelves. Ideally, heavier books, such as coffee table volumes, go on the bottom. Lighter paperbacks should be placed on the top shelves.

WHAT YOU'LL NEED

Time: **45 minutes** | Difficulty: **Medium**

TOOLS:

Pry bar and hammer
Circular saw
Measuring tape
Carpenter's pencil
Power drill and bits
Level

Hammer
Putty knife
Palm sander
Paintbrush

MATERIALS:

1 pallet

2" wood screws
Finish nails
Wood putty
80-grit sandpaper
Primer (optional)
Paint (optional)

HOW YOU MAKE IT

1. Remove the bottom deck boards from a pallet and use a circular saw to cut the top deck boards along one edge of the middle stringer.

2. Set the two-stringer section on its side (resting on a stringer face). Cut two 4½" spacers from scrap. Use the spacers to separate the stringer resting on the surface and a separate deconstructed stringer laid parallel to the first (any notches should face each other).

3. Measure and mark shelf locations, starting with the first 8" up from the bottom. Make subsequent marks across both stringers at 21 ½", 34½", and 47¼". These marks represent the top edges of the shelf cleats.

4. Cut and rip eight shelf cleats 1¾" wide by 10½" long from stringers. Align the top edge of the first cleat with the 8" line, so that the back edge is flush with the back of the rear stringer (the stringer with the deck boards attached). Screw the cleat across the stringers with 2" wood screws. Repeat the process with cleats at the remaining three marks.

5. Lay the bookshelves on the opposite side and repeat the process to construct the second bookshelf side. Stand the bookshelf up and check for level and plumb. Adjust the stringer legs as necessary.

6. Check level across the brackets and adjust as necessary. Starting at the top, dry lay three shelf boards 17¾" long, cut from deck boards, across the top cleats (there should be a gap at the front of the shelves). Drill pilot holes and fasten the shelves to the cleats with finish nails. Repeat to install the rest of the shelves.

7. Rip four 2½×17¾" fascia boards from deck boards. Drill pilot holes and fasten the fascia boards in front of the shelves by nailing them to the shelf boards and cleats.

8. Putty over all the nail heads, let dry, and sand smooth. Sand the entire bookshelf, finish natural, or prime and paint in the desired color.

STYLING YOUR BOOKSHELF

If you've gone to the trouble to build a handsome bookshelf, it's a shame to haphazardly pile books on the shelves or just line them up in boring rows. Use the strategies below to spruce up the look of the bookshelves and add visual interest to any room.

• **Stack books vertically and horizontally.** Piles of books can serve as bookends or just break up long, boring rows of books. This is also a good way to store books that are too tall to fit into the shelves vertically.

• **Top stacked books with a candle or other eye-catching bric-a-brac.** This will add even more zest to the look.

• **Intersperse books and photos.** This is a great way to show off photos, even if they've been framed for wall hanging, because you can simply lean them against the back of the bookshelf. For an even more stylish look, dare to lean a small photo in front of the book spines.

• **Incorporate keepsake boxes as heavy decorative additions that also serve a storage purpose.** These can be used to hide away small items like pens, office supplies, and other items that wouldn't necessarily improve the look of the shelves. Match the material of the box—metal, cardboard, wood, or brightly colored plastic—to the look of the shelves.

• **Don't be afraid of blank spaces.** Leaving a strategic gap can be a way of adding a little elegance to the bookshelf. Any gap shouldn't be more than a few inches wide or it risks looking like wasted space.

QUICK 3

Small storage fixtures can have a big impact when they're used in the right places to add ease and comfort to daily living. The truth is, most people don't think to buy simple items like shoe racks and coasters. They just tolerate the inefficiencies, constantly tripping over shoe clutter next to the mudroom door or putting up with water rings on their lovely coffee table. It's a shame, because these small annoyances are so easily avoidable. What's more, crafting these small amenities is almost instantaneous gratification. You'll save a little bit of money, but you'll also be pleasantly surprised at how much your modest creations get used. One of the best things about small projects such as these, however, is that you can customize them to your hearts delight. It's a small matter to put your own signature on a set of coasters, and if you come up with a really cool look, go ahead and whip out multiples for some wonderful, handmade Christmas gifts. In any case, these three super-simple projects are all exceedingly easy and can be fabricated in minutes. Those may be the best minutes you spend in your workshop.

1. SHOE RACK

You can find a variety of shoe racks at retail, in a range of materials from plastic to wood. But maybe you want totally customizable, durable, and easy-to-make shoe shelves for a mudroom, backdoor stoop, or other

rough-and-tumble space. No problem. Pallet wood is meant for getting dirty. Remove the bottom boards from a pallet and use a circular saw to cut the top deck boards along one edge of the center stringer. Cut the two-stringer section twelve inches long, and cut additional shoe rack levels to match from the rest of the pallet. One of the great features of these shoe racks is that it's easy to make multiples. Stack them up for a short tower of shoes that can sit right beside a door. Or set them side by side so that they fit nicely under a mudroom bench. In any case, a bench or other type of seating is the perfect partner to these shoe racks (and don't forget to add the wall-mounted **Coat Rack** on page 76). Have a large family, busy house, or huge mudroom? You can cut a full pallet into sections twelve inches long, for wider shoe shelves. Whatever you build, wood pallet shoe racks are rarely finished in any way because they take so much punishment over their working life that the look would quickly be destroyed.

2. UTENSIL HOLDER

Chances are that when it comes time to find that spatula to turn your pancakes, you have to scrounge through a kitchen draw and disentangle it from a bunch of other utensils and kitchen aids. You can certainly buy ceramic or high-end wood utensil holders, but they are usually fairly expensive for something that serves such a basic function. Most people just do without, putting up with the near-constant frustration of muddled utensils in an overstuffed drawer. Well, no more. Cut a three-and-a-half-inch-long section of deck board to make a square. Cut a separate deck board into quarters, each ten inches long. Use construction glue and finish nails (drill pilot holes first!) to fasten the "walls" to the square base, and butt join the walls to each other. You can finish

the structure natural or create a distressed look that will fit right into a country kitchen. For a little added decorative appeal, cut a pattern of different sized holes in each wall with hole saws and drill bits. Make multiples to hold different types of utensils if you're an avid cook, and if you come up with a particularly striking design, go ahead and make presents for friends who will surely appreciate the thoughtful kitchen addition.

3. DRINK COASTERS

These simple, quick, and easy-to-make eye-catchers are not only a great addition to your home, they also make fantastic gifts. Cut three-and-a-half-inch squares from deck boards and sand them well. Make a pattern of small indentations with a drill to create visual interest and wick away any moisture, or cut a light circle into the surface of each coaster with a hole saw. Then finish or paint as desired, using matte paint or stain. The variations you can create are almost endless. Cut different shapes such as hexagons by using a jigsaw instead of a hole saw. Or use a jigsaw to cut each coaster into a unique oval or other unusual shape. You can paint the coasters in vibrant colors, but it makes more sense to stain them and avoid any sealing finishes—the coaster should be left porous to absorb liquids and condensation. You can also stencil witty images or even words onto each coaster for a truly unique look.

SPICE RACK

Everybody has one. That one shelf in a cupboard where you keep spices, many of which you don't even realize you have. They're jammed in, one in front of the other, making finding the spice you need a matter of pulling every single spice jar out of the cupboard—and then putting them all back again once you're done.

That's why the ideal place for spices is in a rack where it's easy to see the jar you need and all the jars are kept neat, tidy, and organized. In other words, a rack like the one in this project.

This is a small project that requires a good bit of sawing, but is otherwise not a challenge to assemble. However, the measurements do need to be precise in such a small construction. Errors can quickly be magnified, so be careful as you work.

The rack is meant to be screwed to a wall, but it will also sit comfortably under a cabinet on a countertop. The idea is always to make the spices as conveniently located as possible for wherever you do most of your cooking or baking.

This rack has been stained, but you may prefer to paint yours white or leave it natural. Before choosing how you're going to finish it, consider that something this small on a wall in the kitchen is really a design accent. Don't be afraid to experiment with brighter colors that complement the existing color scheme in your kitchen.

WHAT YOU'LL NEED

Time: **20 minutes** | Difficulty: **Easy**

TOOLS:

Circular saw or table saw

Speed square

Measuring tape

Carpenter's pencil

Bar clamp

Power drill and bits

Hammer

Sanding block

2" paintbrush

Torpedo level

MATERIALS:

1 pallet

2" finish nails

Wood putty

100-grit sandpaper

Stain or paint

HOW YOU MAKE IT

1. Cut two sides 19½" long and three top and back braces 13" long from deck boards.

2. Lay the two sides next to each other on their faces, so that they are perfectly aligned. Use a speed square to make a mark on each board 6¼" from the bottom end of the side pieces and another 6¼" up from that mark.

3. Clamp the sides to the top so that the top is flush on both ends. Drill pilot holes and fasten the sides to the top with finish nails.

4. Lay one back brace under the top, flat between the sides. Lay the second with its top edge aligned with the first mark up from the bottom. Drill pilot holes through the sides into the edges of the braces and nail the sides to the braces with finish nails.

5. Rip and cut three shelves 2¾" wide by 13" long from deck boards. Rip and cut three fronts from deck boards, 1½" wide. Position the bottom shelf flush with the bottom of the sides. Position the other two shelves flush with the shelf marks (the back edges of all three should be flush with the backs of the sides). Fasten them in place as you did the top.

6. Nail the shelf fronts perpendicular to the shelves, with the front boards' bottom edges flush with the bottom of the shelves.

7. Conceal the nail heads with wood putty, let it dry, and sand the unit all over before painting it (or staining it if you prefer). Choose a location, and drive screws through the back boards into studs or anchors, checking to ensure level before tightening them all the way down.

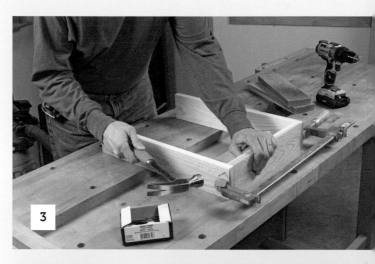

ROLLING TOY BIN

If you have children, you've no doubt experienced the pain of stepping on a toy car barefoot on your way to the bathroom in the dark, or witnessed firsthand the clutter bomb any child's room can become. Kids inevitably accumulate lots and lots of toys, and kids being kids, they aren't generally concerned with where those toys wind up.

If you have any hope of getting ahead of clutter in a house that includes children, you'll need useful toy storage that kids can use instinctively and that will go where the clutter is. A rolling toy bin fills the bill nicely.

The trick to teaching children of any age to clean up after themselves is providing storage that the child doesn't even need to think about. Lining up a zoo's worth of stuffed animals on one shelf of a bookcase is probably not going to happen. But throwing the stuffed animals into a bin? That's more appealing to a child. And that's why the lid was purposely left off this rolling bin. The less kids need to do to put toys away, the more likely they are to actually put them away.

The size and shape of the bin in this project aren't an accident. The container is large enough to accommodate most small toys, yet small enough not to get in the way. The wheels make it incredibly easy for children to drag the bin to where the mess is— yet another feature that will aid cleanup.

You can leave the bin natural, but painting it a bright and lively color is a good idea, not only because the look suits a child's room, but also because you want the bin to be easy for kids to see (yet another thing that will make them more likely to use it).

The bin may prove so useful that you make multiples for different types of toys. Given the ease of construction, that shouldn't be a problem. And keep in mind that this handy storage unit can be repurposed once your children have grown. You can sand off the paint and put it to work in a garage as a portable dolly for tools and supplies. Or stain it and use it in a mudroom to hold foul-weather gear.

TOOLS:

Circular saw or table saw

Power drill and bits

Measuring tape

Carpenter's pencil

Palm sander

Paintbrush

MATERIALS:

1 pallet

1 ½" wood screws

3" wood screws

2" wood screws

100-grit sandpaper

1 quart paint

(4) 1 ¼" casters

HOW YOU MAKE IT

1. Cut six floorboards 14" long from deck boards. Lay two as bottom braces parallel and 7" apart. Line the four remaining boards on top and perpendicular to the braces. Ensure the braces are flush with the outside of the floorboards. Screw the floorboards to the braces with 1½" wood screws.

2. Cut four 12" studs from a stringer. Measure and mark the location of the studs on each corner of the floor, ¾" in from each edge. Screw the studs in place with 3" wood screws driven from the underside of the floor and braces.

3. Measure and mark the wallboard locations on all the studs' outside edges and faces. Make the first marks 3½" up from the bottom, and make a second set 4¼" up from the first.

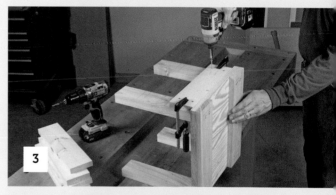

4. Cut six 14"-long wallboards and six 12½" long from deck boards. Starting at the bottom of one wall, screw the short wallboards in place flush with the marks on the studs, with the board ends flush with the stud faces, using 2" wood screws. Repeat on the opposite wall.

5. Repeat the process with the long boards, overlapping the short boards. Drill pilot holes and screw the long boards to the short boards with 1½" wood screws on each side.

6. Use a palm sander to smooth the toy bin all over, and then paint it your desired color. Screw a caster in each corner of the bottom.

4 FURNISHINGS & DÉCOR

The innate strength and durability of pallet wood comes into its own used as furnishings and in decorative accents inside the home. Something meant to hold up to the rough-and-tumble of moving canned goods thousands of miles in the back of a bouncing truck can surely hold up to life as your bed, coffee table, or even a kitchen island.

What might be more surprising, though, is just how well pallets and the wood they're made of work for creating smaller, more decorative home furnishings. You can create a wonderful mirror frame, tea light holders, a clock, or a bathmat from the same wood that was the lumber equivalent of a teamster. The beauty of this chapter is the diversity of projects, ranging between those larger furnishings and the smaller, attractive accent pieces. There's something in this chapter for every room in the home and every taste or need.

PLATFORM BED

A comfortable bed is one of life's great luxuries. Although we think of the mattress as the key to comfort, mattresses are just one part of the equation. The best beds provide a solid foundation that doesn't feel like it might collapse under you as you toss and turn during the night. The bed should also support the mattress in a way that will ensure the greatest longevity of the mattress, because mattresses are anything but cheap. Fortunately, you can save a nice little chunk of change with a pallet bed like the one in this project. You'd be hard pressed to find a bed more secure and simple to construct than this platform.

The design of this bed is unconventional and lends a modern, almost industrial look to a bedroom (although the bed itself can be entirely concealed with oversized blankets or comforters). It's an exceedingly simple look that you can dress up in a number of ways, from painting the pallets to siding them with a custom-made fabric "skirt."

No matter what you think of the look, though, there's no disputing that the construction of this project is perfect for the amazingly popular proliferation of memory foam mattresses. Unlike box spring sets that require only side rails for support, memory foam mattresses call for a firm foundation with closely spaced slats. The gaps between slats allow for air circulation that will help combat mildew and dust mites, and a platform bed like this eliminates annoying squeaks and sounds common to rail frames and less sturdy slatted beds.

The design in this project is sized to accommodate a standard queen-size mattress, although it can support a king-size unit if you're willing to give up some of the border space on the platform. A smaller double or twin mattress will look lost on the platform though.

One of the wonderful things about this bed is that it's so easy to assemble. Because the bed sits flat on the floor it is relatively self-leveling, and there are no precise measurements to take in the fabrication process. You also won't need any special skills or tools. You can make the process even easier by nailing, rather than screwing, the pallets together (just use more nails). As a bonus, it's almost risk-free. If you find that the bed isn't to your liking, it can easily be deconstructed and the pallets reused in another project.

PICKING THE RIGHT MATTRESS

The beauty of a platform bed like this is that you don't need a box spring, which potentially saves you a good bit of money. However, depending on the type of mattress you select, you can easily eat up that savings. Manufacturers are increasingly offering hybrids, such as mattresses that pair an innerspring core with a memory foam top, but the market is still dominated by sales of the individual types listed here.

• **Innerspring.** This is the traditional mattress, usually paired with a box spring that is mounted on a traditional metal rail frame. But the mattress will last just as long and perform just as well on the slatted surface of a pallet platform bed like the one in this project. Quality among innerspring mattresses varies wildly. A bare unit with minimal padding over the spring core will cost little more than $100 and can be expected to be comfortable for five years at most. A luxury "pillow-top" mattress with thick padding and a heavy-duty frame may carry a twenty-year warranty and a price tag close to $1,000. There are a wealth of options in between.

• **Foam.** The most recent innovation in mattress technology, memory foam units continue to grow in popularity. The thickness and type of foam (most companies use proprietary formulas) determine comfort, longevity, and price. At the high end of the spectrum, these mattresses can run thousands of dollars and offer a premium sleep experience. But even at the budget end, these miracles of modern technology offer sleep comfort most people find superior. Foam mattresses are ideal for a pallet platform bed because the technology actually requires the mattress be placed on a slatted surface with gaps, rather than a solid platform. The weight also ensures that the mattress moves around on the platform less than an innerspring or air mattress would.

• **Air.** Air mattresses can be adjusted to suit your preferred firmness, and they are the least expensive among the options listed here. However, they are also the least comfortable and tend to make noises as you move during sleep. They are the least desirable option because they are prone to movement and the pallet platform bed in this project doesn't include channels or fences to hold a mattress in place.

• **Futon.** A time-tested type of simple mattress formed of layers of batting surrounded by a durable canvas body, futons are an acquired taste. The surface is softer than a floor, but harder than any other mattress type. Futons are relatively inexpensive and, because of their simple construction, can last decades. Used on a pallet platform bed, they raise the top level of the bed only a couple of inches, so if you choose a futon, be sure the bed as you've built it is at the height you prefer.

WHAT YOU'LL NEED

Time: 1.5 hours | Difficulty: **Easy**

TOOLS:

Pry bar

Palm sander

Paintbrush (optional)

Hammer

Power drill and screw bits

MATERIALS:

8 pallets

100-grit sandpaper

Primer (optional)

White gloss enamel paint (optional)

3" wood screws

(14) 4" zinc mending plates and screws

4" wood screws

Self-adhesive felt furniture pads

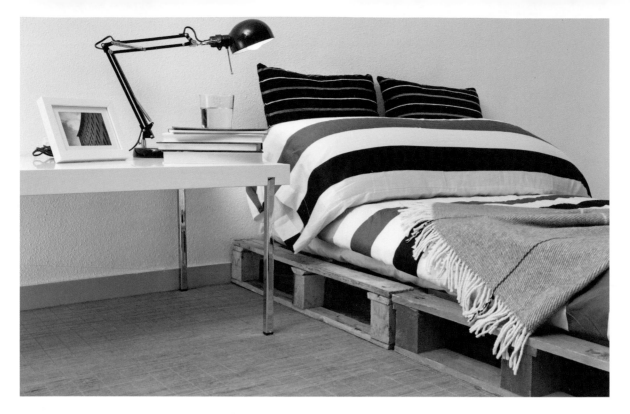

This simple twin-size bed was formed by simply nailing unfinished pallets together to form one long, narrow surface. The futon mattress is tough enough to withstand the occasional splinter, and the bed took little effort and only a few minutes to make. This is the perfect space-efficient, dorm-room bedding solution.

You don't necessarily need to build a base layer for the platform bed to get it to a comfortable height. This home crafter created a top layer of four pallets and strategically placed wood bolsters underneath as a foundation that allows for increased air circulation and easier cleaning under the bed.

HOW YOU MAKE IT

1. Remove the bottom deck boards from eight standard pallets. Smooth the pallets all over with a palm sander, so that no rough spots or splinters remain.

2. If you're painting the bed, prime and paint the pallets all over. You can paint them any color, but white is the most common and the least likely to go out of style. If you don't like white, gray or very pale blue or green would work for most bedrooms.

3. Set four pallets in a grid, laying upside-down on the top deck boards, with the stringers running from what will be the foot of the bed to the head (notched edges up). Fasten the two pallets together, side by side at the head of the bed, with 3" wood screws. Drive screws every few inches, alternating sides.

4. Repeat the process with the two pallets at the foot of the bed. Fasten the stringers of the foot pallets to the head pallet stringers with 4" zinc mending plates screwed to both sides of each stringer pair. Reinforce the connection by screwing mending plates at the center point of the deck boards (on the underside) across the pallets.

5. Build the base layer on top of the first layer, notched edge up, with the remaining four pallets fastened in exactly the same way.

6. Alternating sides, drive 4" wood screws down through the stringers of the top layer, into the stringers of the layer below. Attach self-adhesive felt furniture pads every 3" along the bottom of each top stringer.

7. Use a helper to flip the bed and position it in its final location. Check for any splinters or rough spots before sitting the mattress on top of the bed frame.

KITCHEN ISLAND

A kitchen island can be the perfect center-piece to a busy kitchen. Providing both readily accessible storage and much-needed uncluttered workspace, an island is usually an incredibly handy addition to the room. The island in this project is a perfect example of this kitchen standard at its functional best. It features a basic but entirely usable design that will make whipping up meals a breeze.

Although most islands are manufactured with single-surface tops, this one features a slatted work surface that is both easier to build and supportive of a number of kitchen prep duties, such as cooling pies or working with multiple mixing bowls to create a complex recipe. However, you may find it useful to add a large cutting board with a lip or some other solid surface for prepping wet or crumbly foods.

As simple as this island is, the look is understated and handsome. That means it will fit right in with just about any kitchen décor. You can also add to the function and the look of the island by outfitting it with hooks or magnetic strips to hold pans, utensils, or kitchen cutlery. You can add casters to make the island mobile, something that is a must in a large kitchen. If you're looking for a more finished appearance, don't hesitate to use this island as a skeleton base for finish materials such as plywood panels and a butcher-block top. Enclose it on three sides and it will look more traditional, and you can finish the panels to match the walls of the kitchen or your bottom cabinets.

Whatever look or modification you opt for, keep in mind that this is a food prep surface, so any finish must be food safe. A simple coating of tung or linseed oil will bring the beauty of the wood out and help keep the slats and other members from drying out for a long time to come.

ISLAND PLACEMENT

There is a reason kitchen islands are called "islands"; they are positioned so that they are accessible from all sides. The island can serve as a primary work surface, which means it has to be in proper relation to the sink, refrigerator, and stove. Most designers stipulate that the kitchen must be at least eight feet deep and twelve feet long to properly accommodate an island. Here are some other guidelines for placing your island so that it is as functional and handy as possible.

• Islands should never encroach on refrigerator or base cabinet door swing, or on the dishwasher door arc.

• It's best for work safety and efficiency to dedicate a light above the island's surface. The ideal lighting is dimmable and can be adjusted directionally. Pendant lights should hang no lower than thirty inches above the island's work surface (the same is true of a vent hood, if you have one over the island).

• Leave at least thirty-six inches (but preferably forty-two inches) of space for traffic flow around the island. The best kitchen layouts for this spacing are U- or L-shaped kitchens.

• The space between refrigerator, cooktop, sink, and island should be between four and nine feet.

WHAT YOU'LL NEED

Time: **1 hour** | Difficulty: **Medium**

TOOLS:

Pry bar
Circular saw or table saw
Hammer
Power drill and bits
Measuring tape

Carpenter's pencil
Palm sander

MATERIALS:

3 pallets
Finish nails

(4) 6" FastenMaster HeadLok screws
3" wood screws
2" wood screws
100-grit sandpaper
Food-safe finish (optional)

HOW YOU MAKE IT

1. Remove the bottom deck boards from a pallet. Cut the top deck boards along one edge of the center stringer; then deconstruct the two-stringer section and remove the boards and all fasteners. Rip both stringers to 1½" wide to remove the notched sections, and reconstruct the section with the boards evenly spaced and tacked to the stringers with finish nails.

2. Cut two end boards 17¾" long from stringers. Rip them down to 1½" wide to remove the notched sections. Nail them between the ends of the stringers with finish nails to complete the island's top frame.

3. Cut ten top boards 20¾" from deck boards. Space them out along the top between the two end boards, using ½" spacers between them to maintain even spacing. (Two spaces will be ¼" larger, or you can spread all the spacing out slightly).

4. Drill two pilot holes at each end of each deck board and use finish nails to fasten the boards to the stringers.

5. Cut four 35" legs from stringers. Measure and mark a line 15" from the bottom of the legs. This represents the top of the bottom shelf cross braces. Drill and countersink holes from the outside edges of the legs for 6" HeadLok self-tapping screws. Cut the 38" bottom shelf braces from stringers, and fasten the legs to the braces with the screws, with any notches facing down.

6. Attach the legs inside each corner of the frame, the top edges flush with the top of the frame and any notches facing out. Screw the frame to the legs with three 3" wood screws per leg.

7. Cut nine bottom shelf boards 17¾" from deck boards. Space them ¾" apart on the shelf braces and screw them to the braces with 2" screws.

8. Sand the island smooth all over and finish with a food-safe finish such as boiled linseed oil, or leave natural if you prefer.

PALLET PLAY STRUCTURES

Every so often, pallet seekers come across a treasure trove. It can be a dumpster overflowing with pallets that a construction company makes clear they aren't going to reclaim or recycle. Or maybe a local discount store goes out of business, leaving behind an untidy tower of old pallets they are just hoping goes away. Wherever they come from, when you salvage a large quantity of pallets, you take what you get. There may be some mismatched sizes, and several of the pallets may be slightly (or more than slightly) damaged. Whatever the case, reclaiming a large number of pallets is equal parts work and reward. All of the pallets will require a thorough cleaning before use, and you'll want to sand or otherwise treat defects and areas that might lead to splinters.

You can use the pallets for any of the projects in this book or others of your own design, but a large collection of pallets begs to be used for something that will benefit specifically from the abundance. A yard or play structure is ideal, because it can be built from unmodified pallets and can be designed to use up a large inventory.

Using pallets for building structures makes sense. There is natural strength and durability in the structure of the pallets, because the deck boards are usually attached to the stringers or blocks with incredibly strong fasteners. The downside is that, when left in their original form, the pallets have gaps in their surfaces. There are many ways to deal with that issue. In some cases, as with a playhouse that will only be used during the day and in good weather, the gaps simply don't matter. If you're hoping to use the structure in inclement weather, or just want a truly enclosed space, you can cut and rip deck boards to fill in the spaces on the pallets you're using, or staple plastic sheeting or another barrier on the inside walls and ceiling of the structure.

The bigger challenge is the design of the structure you want to build. Using pallets whole to build any kind of a structure requires careful planning. You should draft a design on grid paper, measuring the pallets to ensure everything fits as planned. Then, it's just a matter of executing the design for the structure you want to build.

• Playhouses. Start with the foundation. Clear a space slightly larger than the footprint of the playhouse. Dig down a couple inches, if you're okay with the foundation sitting above ground level. Otherwise, excavate six inches and lay down a one-inch layer of gravel; the top of the foundation will be roughly level with the surrounding ground. Create the foundation by screwing stringers together with four-inch

deck screws. Use more screws than you think you need, to ensure the integrity of the foundation. Single pallets can be used for the walls and can be screwed directly to the foundation by laying pallets stringer face down and screwing the walls in place. In most cases, a flat roof will do just fine.

Although a pallet playhouse won't look as finished as the units offered at retail, there are advantages over prefab playhouses and more involved playhouse plans. A crude structure such as this allows kids to use their imaginations to pretend the structure is whatever they want it to be—from a castle to a three-bedroom bungalow.

The rough-and-tumble nature of the structure is perfect for play. Children can mark up, beat on, or just abuse the structure all they want without worrying about being punished. They can use it as a chance to express themselves with crayons, paint, or other materials that wouldn't be welcome inside the house or in a more formal, prefab playhouse.

• Treehouses. The base is key in any elevated structure, and no more so than in a treehouse. The challenge is to design the treehouse to accommodate an existing tree. Keep in mind

that the closer the house is to the ground, the safer it is. But in any case, the most stable platform for a treehouse is one that is supported by the crotch formed between the trunk and a branch or branches. To ensure absolute stability, fasten base pallets to one another and to the tree. It's wise to use lag screws or similar fasteners, because there's no such thing as overkill when constructing a treehouse base. You'll also want to check for level several times as you work.

You can use the base as a simple platform to enjoy quiet time in the tree, but in most cases it makes more sense to construct at least rudimentary walls to ensure nobody falls off the platform. Craft a more involved structure for youngsters who want an elevated clubhouse, but keep in mind that safety is key. Walls should be kept low. If you're going to construct taller walls, it's wise to sandwich pallets, creating strong, double-thick walls. However, any structure you create in a tree also has to be as lightweight as possible.

To enclose the walls or the ceiling, use the thinnest exterior plywood you can find and clad the outside of the structure in the plywood sheets.

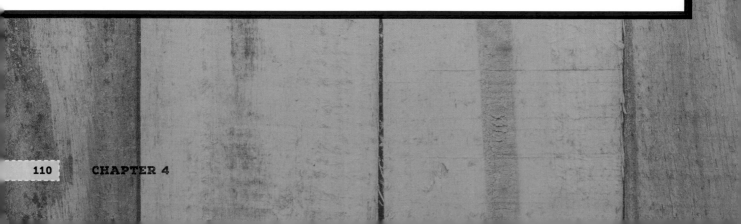

BAR STOOL

Despite the name, this tall chair can be used even if you don't have a breakfast bar or an actual wet bar. It can be handy additional seating kept around the margins of a living room or kitchen, serve as a solid resting place in a workshop, or provide seating in other places throughout the home.

However, the stool was specifically designed with a size that best fits under the average height of a high counter. It's meant to sit perfectly under the lip of a breakfast bar, leaving plenty of room for your legs and general movement. That said, you can always adjust the height of the stool by cutting the legs down for a lower counter. Just make sure to adjust the placement of the bottom aprons accordingly (or eliminate them entirely if you're cutting the legs down dramatically to use the stool as a simple chair).

The stool is also designed with a slanted back for maximum comfort. As it is, the lower aprons serve as footrests, because, unless you're very tall, your feet aren't going to reach the floor when you're sitting on the stool. For even more comfort, consider adding a seat cushion.

In most cases, a single stool isn't going to cut it; there's usually room for three or more stools at a breakfast bar or in front of a standalone den bar. If you're planning on making more than one of these, it only makes sense to construct them all at once. That way, you can save time and effort by using cut pieces as templates to mark other pieces and ganging cutting and fabrication steps for all the stools.

WHAT YOU'LL NEED

Time: **1 hour** | Difficulty: **Medium**

TOOLS:

Circular saw or table saw
Measuring tape
Carpenter's pencil
Metal straightedge
Pocket hole jig
Power drill and bits

Hammer
Palm sander
Paintbrush (optional)

MATERIALS:

2 pallets
2 ½" pocket hole screws

2" wood screws
Finish nails
Wood putty
100-grit sandpaper
Paint or finish (optional)

HOW YOU MAKE IT

1. Cut two front legs 31¾" long from stringers. Measure and mark the faces of two additional stringers with a line 31¾" from one end. Mark the opposite end 1½" in from the edge. Use a straightedge to connect the two marks on each stringer. Use a circular saw to cut the angled seatback.

2. Cut two seat frame sides 12" long and two fronts 13½" long from stringers. Rip the frame pieces down to 2¾".

3. Use a pocket hole jig to drill two pocket holes on each end of the frame pieces.

4. Construct one leg pair by screwing a side frame piece to the front and back legs, with the pieces face down on a work surface. Use 2½" pocket hole screws. The top of the frame side should be flush with the 31¾" mark on the back leg and the top of the front leg.

5. Cut four aprons 18" long and four 19" long from deck boards. Measure and mark lines 10" up the legs from the bottom of one leg pair. Use 2" wood screws to fasten a short apron across the legs, the top aligned with the marks and the edges aligned with the outside edges of the legs. Repeat with the opposite leg pair.

6. Screw a front frame piece between the front legs with 2½" pocket hole screws. Screw the rear frame piece in place, the top aligned with the 31¾" marks on the back legs.

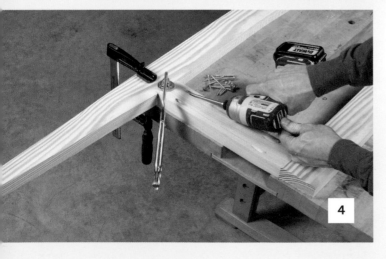

7. Align the lower front apron with lower side aprons, overlapping their ends. Screw the front apron to the front legs with 2" wood screws. Fasten the lower rear apron in the same way. Drill pilot holes at the ends of the front and back aprons and nail those aprons to the side aprons with finish nails.

8. Align the bottom of the upper side aprons with the bottom of the frame (they will project above the front leg tops by ¾" or however thick the deck boards you're using are). Screw them to the legs with 2" wood screws. Fasten the front and rear aprons in the same way, measuring them to be sure they overlap the side aprons flush on each side.

9. Cut eight seat slats 16½" long from deck boards. Butt the first seat slat front edge against the inside of the front apron, drill pilot holes, and nail the slat to the side frame with finish nails. Continue fastening the seat slats to the frame, leaving about a ⅛" gap between slats.

10. Position and fasten the seatback slats the same way, starting at the top edge of the back legs and working down toward the seat.

11. Putty over exposed nail and screw heads and sand smooth. Use a palm sander and 100-grit sandpaper to smooth the stool all over, and finish or paint as desired.

SPACE INVADER

Crafting the perfect bar stool is a matter of sizing it correctly to fit properly with the bar or counter at which it will be placed. To measure correctly for a bar stool, measure from the floor to the bottom of the counter or bar. That height should be approximately ten inches more than the height from the bottom of the legs to the top of the stool seat.

• **Height.** Bar stool heights range from thirty to thirty-six inches. The height should correspond to the height of your bar or counter, which usually ranges from forty to forty-six inches.

Spacing. Stool spacing is also important to ensure comfort. Ideally, there should be twenty-eight inches from the center of one stool to the center of the stool next to it. Stools should be at least fourteen inches on center from a wall or the end of a counter. This allows people room to freely move their arms while eating or drinking on the stools.

QUICK 3

Some pallet creations bridge the gap between furniture, structure, and safety feature. These divide or connect spaces and can actually serve vital roles. The three options included here not only define the space in a home; they are also simple projects to construct because they use pallets whole or relatively whole. Each of these features a simple design that won't require much in the way of fabrication skill, effort, or expensive tools to assemble. All are innovative applications that can be used purely for function or spruced up as decorative architectural elements. Just keep in mind that these are all related to home safety, so it's imperative that you be careful when constructing and installing them to ensure they don't cause harm where they were meant to ensure against it.

1. CHILD'S SAFETY GATE

Safety gates are essential to keep toddlers corralled and to prevent them from venturing up or down stairs, or careening around a busy kitchen. But plastic gates can be pricey and look, well, slightly cheesy. Create your own safety gate by cutting the deck boards along one edge of the pallet, and then cut the two-stringer section to match the opening you need to secure. This process is a simple one that only requires careful measuring. That said,

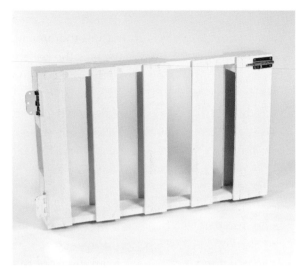

you'll also need to smooth the surface of the cut pallet all over to ensure that there is no area on which a child could get a splinter or cut himself. Finish the gate as you prefer (consider a fun, primary color design to amuse the little one). To complete the gate, screw sturdy hinges onto the stringer ends at one side, and fasten a gate latch tongue (one half of the gate latch) to the opposite end of one stringer. Position the gate in the space where you need it, check for level and mounting height, and mark for the gate latch receiver. Screw the hinges to one side of the opening and the receiver to the opposite side. Test the gate's operation and make adjustments as necessary.

2. PALLET STAIRCASE

Pallets can make surprisingly good staircases for lofts, treehouse platforms, or other unusual elevated areas. The idea is to stack the pallets in a staggered formation, with adequate support underneath the upper pallets. Low staircases of four or five steps are best to maintain integrity. The most basic straight staircase can be built on a platform of three or four full pallets screwed together, with decreasing pallet platforms on each successive level, creating a jagged right triangle when viewed from the side. You can also build a staircase from pallets stacked one atop the other, with each successive pallet ten inches back from the front of the one below it (which will require adequate support for the upper-step pallets). Screw the pallets together through their stringers with six-inch lag screws. Support the upper pallets with beams or stacked concrete blocks. Secure the topmost pallet to the upper platform with lag screws. You can even build an L staircase by crafting a transition platform of a pallet or four pallets. This will require much more support. Whenever you build a structural feature such as a staircase, safety is paramount. If you have any doubts about the support needed, consult a structural engineer and the local building department.

3. PALLET ROOM DIVIDER SCREEN

Pallets make excellent room dividers because they visually separate different areas while still allowing for air and light penetration. Build individual walls for the divider by setting a pallet on a stringer face and then screwing a second pallet on top of the first (if you just want a knee-wall divider, you won't need the top pallet). Connect successive divider sections with three-inch marine hinges attached to the stringer ends. Use large, round, self-adhesive furniture pads under each wall to prevent the stringers from scratching floors. Using this method will take less than an hour to construct a bi-fold or tri-fold screen. Be aware that the screen will be heavier than most room dividers, and you should enlist the assistance of a helper in moving the screen. The real fun in this project is decorating the divider. You can simply sand, prep, and paint a pallet divider in color schemes to complement or contrast your décor. For even more flair, staple fabric panels over one or both sides of the walls to create a true privacy screen. Stencil or screen images onto the deck boards to make the screen a focal point of any room, or use it as a display wall for a group of framed photos or even for a favorite piece of framed art.

DOG BED

If you really care about your canine family member, you'll give the furry napper a place to lie down. It's not just a matter of being good to your pet; veterinarians recommend that dogs have their own bed to sleep in. Getting a dog off a cold floor helps him sleep better and stay healthier. It's especially beneficial for older dogs, because cold or uncomfortably hard floors can aggravate older bones and joints.

This particular bed is designed with three side walls. In addition to the benefits any dog bed offers, the walls create a sense of security for the dog, helping him sleep better.

The design is also large. That's a good thing because it allows a dog to spread out; dogs tend to move a lot when they sleep. This bed is ideal for dogs from small to large, skinny to chubby. Whatever the size of your dog, you should add a mattress and a dog blanket to make the bed as comfortable as possible.

One of the great features of using pallet wood for a dog bed is its cleanability. Keep that in mind if you decide to decorate the bed or paint it. It would be wiser to use gloss paint rather than flat, and, obviously, you should stay away from any toxic finishes that the dog might lick.

WHAT YOU'LL NEED

Time: **30 minutes** | Difficulty: **Easy**

TOOLS:

Reciprocating saw
Circular saw or table saw
Power drill and bits
Measuring tape
Carpenter's pencil
Palm sander

MATERIALS:

1 pallet

3" wood screws
2" wood screws
80-grit sandpaper

HOW YOU MAKE IT

1. Carefully remove the bottom deck boards and the center stringer from a pallet using a reciprocating saw to sever the fasteners and leave the top deck boards intact. Use a circular saw to cut five posts from the removed stringer, each 9" long.

2. Turn the modified pallet upside down, so that the deck boards are on the bottom and any notches on the stringers are facing up. Screw deck boards across the exposed ends of the stringers, using 3" wood screws.

3. Screw a post into each corner with the edges toward the stringers. Measure 24" in from the edge of what will be the rear bed stringer, and mark this center point. Center the face of the remaining post on this mark, and screw it to the stringer with 3" wood screws.

4. Cut two side walls 38½" long from deck boards. Screw them to the posts on either side with 2" wood screws. The wall should be flush with the edges and tops of the posts.

5. Cut two 24" back boards from deck boards, and fasten each between a back post and the back center post, securing them with 2" wood screws.

6. Sand the bed lightly all over. Leave it natural as with the bed shown here, or finish or paint the bed as you prefer. Add a pet mattress and your pet's favorite toys.

MIRROR FRAME WITH SHELF

Every entryway should have its own mirror. Nobody wants to head out of the house with a cowlick or a big piece of lettuce between their teeth. An entryway mirror is your last chance to make a good first impression on the rest of the world. This one is even handier than most in that it includes a useful shelf that can hold keys, glasses, a cell phone, and other small items.

This project was designed around a standard mirror available through home centers nationwide. The dimensions are twenty-three and a half inches by thirty-one and a half inches. However, if you can't find that size, you can always use another size and adapt the frame. The inside frame dimensions should be about a one-quarter inch less on all sides than the dimensions of your mirror.

WHAT YOU'LL NEED

Time: **45 minutes** | Difficulty: **Medium**

TOOLS:

Circular saw
Pocket hole jig
Power drill and bits
Router or table saw

Measuring tape
Carpenter's pencil
Palm sander

MATERIALS:

1 pallet

1 ¼" pocket hole screws
2" wood screws
100-grit sandpaper
³⁄₈"×1-½" metal corner braces
Wire hanger kit

HOW YOU MAKE IT

1. Cut two frame pieces 30¼" long, and two 31¼" long from deck boards. Use a pocket hole jig to drill pocket holes at each end of each piece. Screw the frame together with 1 ¼" pocket hole screws.

2. Use a router to cut a ½"-wide by ¼"-deep rabbet around the inside edge of the frame. Square the four corners with a chisel.

3. Center a full-length deck board across the frame on edge. The top of the board should be flush with one of the long inside edges of the frame. Mark each end of the board for the cuts for the wraparound. Measure ¾" in from the edge at each mark, and make another mark. Draw lines between between each inside mark and edge mark. Drill starter holes at each corner of the marked area, and use a jigsaw to cut out the inset for the shelf.

4. Secure the shelf in position to the frame, and drill pilot holes through the back of the frame and into the shelf's inside edge. Screw the frame to the shelf with 2" wood screws.

5. Sand the mirror all over and finish or paint as desired. Secure the mirror in the rabbet with corner braces. Use a wire hanger kit rated for at least 30 lbs. to attach a wire hanger to the back of the mirror.

RESILVERING MIRRORS

Although you can buy a new mirror to go in the frame in this project, there are advantages to reclaiming an older mirror from a thrift shop, flea market, or other secondhand source. First, a timeworn mirror will perfectly match the naturally rustic nature of the frame, especially if the frame is left unfinished or stained. Second, a secondhand mirror is likely to cost far less than new, increasing the cost benefits that led you to use reclaimed pallet wood in the first place.

Older mirrors can also carry marks of age that are themselves very charming. Most often, the silvering on the back of the mirror—the metallic-based backing that actually makes a piece of glass a mirror—has eroded. This creates phantom black areas that can be alluring.

However, if too much of the silvering is damaged or missing, the mirror ceases to be a functional mirror. In that case, you can resurrect the reflective surface in a process known as "resilvering."

Manufacturers make this process fairly easy by offering efficient silver stripping and resilvering products. Some even sell complete turnkey kits. (You can find these products at home stores and larger hardware or craft stores.) Although using these products is not particularly difficult, they are toxic chemicals that should be used with care, following all the safety precautions on the labels. And although the steps below are the general process for using these types of products, use what you buy in accordance with the manufacturer's instructions to ensure the best final appearance. The process is messy, so make sure you have plenty of space to work on the mirror, and use old work clothes.

1. Assess the glass condition. Flaws or damage to the face of the glass will be accentuated with new silver.

2. Strip the backing. You can do this with a plastic fid or use any of the chemical stripping products available on the market. Follow all safety precautions recommended by the manufacturer. In any case, always wear safety goggles, a respirator, and rubber gloves.

3. Strip the silver. Use a mirror removal product, following the manufacturer's instructions. This usually involves applying the product and then removing the silver (and possibly copper) backing with gauze or cotton balls.

4. Pour tin over the glass, let it sit for about forty seconds, and pour off any excess. Rinse with distilled water. Mix the silver according to the manufacturer's instructions, and then pour the silver evenly over the surface of the glass. The surface will turn brown and then silver. After five minutes, drain any excess silver off the surface of the glass.

5. Let the surface dry completely. Remove any traces of silvering on the face of the mirror by carefully scraping them off with a plastic fid. Reframe the mirror.

When cleaning the face of any antique mirror, spray a lint-free cloth with window cleaner and clean the window with the cloth. Never spray cleaner directly on the face of the glass.

DESK

We all need a good, solid place to work. It doesn't matter if you have a home office or just do your work in a corner of the living room—you need a desk. The best desks are big enough to spread out, forgiving of the occasional meal or cup of coffee during a work session, and are admirably sturdy. All that pretty much describes the desk in this project.

One of the truly great things about this desk is its sheer durability. Although it's a nice enough design to fit right into a living room or other space of the home, it's also tough enough to be a workshop center-piece—a place where you can draft brilliant plans for innovative pallet creations.

The design is actually streamlined, very neat and trim. But it does have a craftsman-style feel and will complement and work with many different types of décor styles.

You can stain or finish the desk as you prefer, but you might want to avoid painting it. A work surface like this looks rather odd when painted.

WHAT YOU'LL NEED

Time: **45 minutes** | Difficulty: **Medium**

TOOLS:

Pry bar
Circular saw or table saw
Palm sander
Power drill and bits
Hammer

Measuring tape
Carpenter's pencil
Level

MATERIALS:

3 pallets

100-grit sandpaper
3" wood screws
2" wood screws
Finish nails
Finish or paint (optional)

HOW YOU MAKE IT

1. Deconstruct two pallets. Cut eleven desktop boards and four aprons 20" long from deck boards. Sand them smooth all around.

2. Cut four legs 25¾" long and two cross braces 38½" long from stringers. (If your stringers have cutouts, buy and cut the legs from clear lumber such as poplar.)

3. Build the leg pairs by screwing each cross brace to the tops of two legs with 3" wood screws. The ends of the brace should be flush with the outside faces of the legs.

4. Place the desktop boards aligned on a flat, level work surface. Sit a leg pair upside down across the boards, on either end, and adjust the boards and the leg pairs so that they are all flush with the ends and edges of the cross braces. Drive 2" wood screws down through the cross brace and into the boards. Repeat the process with the second leg pair.

5. Screw the nine remaining desktop boards in place in the same way, butted tightly together between the two end boards, to complete the desk top.

6. Drill pilot holes and use finish nails to nail the upper side aprons in place, flush with the desktop boards.

7. Measure up from the bottom of the legs 10" and use a level to mark a line on their outside faces at that point. Align the top edge of each lower side apron with the marks, and fasten the aprons in place as you did the upper side aprons.

8. Measure to confirm the length of the front and back deck boards, with a flush overlap of the side aprons. Cut the front and back aprons from deck boards, and drill pilot holes to mount them. Nail them in place. Install the lower back apron in the same way.

9. Sand the desk all over and finish as desired.

FURNITURE LEGS

As handsome as this desk is, you can put your own signature style on it by forming the legs in a unique way. Legs are often the indicators of style for a desk, and this one is no exception.

• **Lathe turning.** Although you'll need both a lathe and the expertise to use it correctly, this is a quick way to modify the bottom sections of the desk legs to a uniform and attractive shape. Picking from a variety of shaping tools, you can add rings or shape the entire leg down to a point. Lathe turning is a great way to form a shape that incorporates the notch as an intentional design element—rather than leaving it as is and risking that it looks a bit accidental.

• **Jigsaw shaping.** Building on the notch to create a more complex profile in the leg is an ideal use of a jigsaw. However, you must be certain that you don't remove so much wood that you compromise the integrity of the leg. Something as simple as a series of small wedges cut out of the edge that includes the notch can make for a repetitive design element that really makes legs stand out. Carefully plan out any jigsaw designs, and transfer all the cuts to the leg with a carpenter's pencil at the same time. That will give you a chance to consider what the entire leg will look like once cut with the shapes.

• **Sanding.** Although it's a slower process that requires a bit more elbow grease, you can build on the shape of a notch in a stringer leg by rounding all the edges and corners, and even sanding undulations in the notched edge of the leg.

• **Replacements.** If you find notches in stringer legs unappealing, or if you just think stringer legs are too blocky a look for your desk, you can opt for aftermarket legs. Cut the legs in this project off right at the bottom of the top surface aprons, and use the cut ends as mounting surfaces for metal hairpin legs (a mid-century modern look) or more conventional turned legs. You'll find these through online sources, and turned legs are widely available at home centers.

HANGING PICTURE FRAME

A picture frame is one of the most useful things you can make from pallet wood. Even small picture frames are pricey, and this one is easy to make and almost free. The nicely mitered corners create a polished appearance that will have guests in your home wondering where you bought such a nice frame.

To make sure that appearance is as pleasing as possible, be careful in measuring and cutting the miters. Be precise and cut the miters with a fine-tooth blade. You might also want to add a hanger on a side and an end frame piece so that you can easily swap the picture for one with a different orientation in the future.

In any case, the frame is a good use of scraps left over from pallet projects. If you're reclaiming a lot of pallets, make sure you keep all the scraps to make frames of different sizes—they make wonderful gifts, and relatives will cherish a family picture inside a handmade frame.

Take as much time choosing a finish as you do crafting the frame. The finish affects not only the look of the frame, but also how the picture will be perceived. You can use a distressed look or just stain the frame to emphasize the wood. But painting the frame is often a wonderful option—black or white will allow the photo inside to grab the most attention.

WHAT YOU'LL NEED

Time: **30 minutes** | Difficulty: **Medium**

TOOLS:

Measuring tape
Carpenter's pencil
Speed square
Table saw
Bar clamps
Putty knife or sanding block
Hammer
Paintbrush

MATERIALS:

1 pallet
Wood glue
Finish nails
80- to 100-grit sandpaper
Wood putty
Stain (optional)
8 x 10" glass pane
Glazier points
Sawtooth frame hangers

HOW YOU MAKE IT

1. Measure and mark the center of two deck boards 10¾" long for frame sides, and the center of 2 deck boards 8¼" long. Mark 45° angles out from the ends of the marks on all boards, to create the miters for the frame (the outside measurements will vary depending on the exact widths of your deck boards).

2. Miter the ends 45°. The interior edges should be 10¾" on the long frame pieces, and 8¼" on the short sides.

3. Use a table saw to cut the rabbets on the inside edge of each frame piece. Make one pass at the outside edge of the rabbet and one for the bottom, to remove the material for the rabbet. As an alternative, use a router table to cut the rabbets.

4. Glue the miter joints and clamp them with bar clamps. Drill pilot holes and nail the frame together through the miter joints with finish nails.

5. Scrape or sand off any glue squeeze-out from the joints. Putty over the nail heads and sand the putty smooth when dry. Distress the frame with gouges or other marks by sandwiching small sharp stones between the frame and a thick piece of cardboard, and shuffling your feet over the cardboard.

6. Stain the frame and let it dry.

7. Have an 8 x 10" piece of glass cut, and cut a piece of thin, stiff cardboard or poster board to match the glass dimensions. Lay the frame flat on its front, and set the glass into the rabbets. Lay the photo on top of the glass, put the cardboard or poster board on top of the photo, and secure the photo and glass in place by tapping a glazier point on each side of the cardboard back, into the edge of the rabbet.

8. Nail a sawtooth hanger centered on the top of the back of the frame (oriented according to the picture). Clean the front of the glass and hang the picture frame.

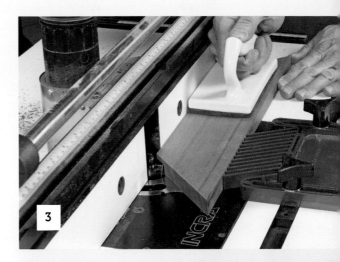

QUICK 3

The sturdy nature of pallets makes for wonderfully chunky and solid furnishings—especially if you're after a rustic look. But you can also manipulate the look of the wood with materials like glossy paint and glass, to create interesting visual combinations or even transform the wood into a more sleek-looking material. The idea is that a piece of pallet furniture is adaptable; it can go modern or industrial, just as easily as it can fit a country-ranch interior. Whatever look you decide on, the truth is that the innate strength of intact pallets makes them a natural for use in furnishings that will be subjected to daily stresses. As anyone who has taken apart a pallet will attest, they are fastened together well to avoid falling apart under rough shipping conditions. Your living room can't begin to re-create the type of stresses pallets are made for. These projects all use whole pallets in unusual ways to create furnishings that might change anybody's mind about the potential for upcycling this shipping standard.

1. COFFEE TABLE

Want an impressive focal point for your living room, one that takes less than twenty minutes of your time and suits all kinds of interior design styles? Look no further. A sleek coffee table is something almost every living room needs, and can be a centerpiece that ties the room's look together. Remove all but the two end deck boards from the bottom of a stringer pallet and then clean up and lightly sand the pallet. Paint it high-gloss white (or another color, as you prefer) and screw four-inch casters to each bottom corner—including at least one locking caster. You can leave the coffee table as is or give it a more polished appearance by having a glass top cut and edge-beveled for a solid top surface (a great idea if you happen to eat in front of the TV a lot, or use your coffee table to hold small

items such as remotes, iPods, or votive candles). Hold the top in place with self-adhesive rubber "dots," available at any hardware store or home center. If you don't have the room for a full-size pallet coffee table, or if you just prefer a more modest unit, you can cut the deck boards along the center stringer to create a more conventional rectangular coffee table that is two stringers wide. Follow the same steps you would with a full-size pallet coffee table.

2. PALLET CHANDELIER

A pallet makes a perfect large rustic candle chandelier for a garden or dining room. Simply sand, prep, and stain the pallet, and then screw in heavy-duty ceiling hooks at each of the four corners on the bottom of the pallet. Screw a pattern of eye hooks into the top of the pallet for hanging votive holders. Then just hang the pallet upside down from joists or other strong supports, using chain and the ceiling hooks. Hang the decorative votive holders from the hooks on the surface of the pallet and you have lovely, soft, romantic lighting whenever you want it. You can, of course, make this a more conventional chandelier for indoor use by wiring several individual corded light sockets from a central ceiling box, and then running the sockets through the gaps in the pallet, securing them to the top deck boards

(which face down when the pallet is hung). The look is industrial and can be modified with the use of clear or half-frosted light bulbs, or even colored bulbs.

3. HEADBOARD

Creating a sturdy, unique headboard wherever you need it couldn't be easier, with the help of a couple of pallets. Stand the pallets on end and screw them together through the stringers along one edge, using 3" wood screws. Decorate the surface that will be facing out as you prefer—try stenciling words onto the deck boards, painting the deck boards different shades of the same color, or just finishing them with an ebony stain. The headboard can just be sandwiched between the head of a platform bed frame and the wall (such as the **Platform Bed** on page 102), or you can attach hooks for a metal-rail box-spring frame. Keeping in mind that whole pallets are the easiest to manipulate and use, you open up a range of other headboard possibilities if you're willing to consider deconstructing pallets and using the loose members. Use three stringers as two side and one center posts, nailing deck boards across the faces of the stringers in a staggered pattern with the deck boards butted edge to edge, and you create a solid headboard that can be decorated with paint, stencils, or screened images.

SIDE TABLE

Side tables are the forgotten players in living rooms, family rooms, and elsewhere. They are, however, wonderful and useful additions to the design of any room. They inevitably have a modest footprint that takes up little floor space, while still providing a top surface exactly where you need it for an accent lamp, a place to put a drink, or a resting ground for magazines or the TV remote.

Like all good side tables, this one has been designed for simplicity of construction and pure durability. The finished height is ideal for use alongside either a couch or a bed. It's also just the right size as a complement to a reading chair in a sunny corner of a room.

The design is handsome, but not so distinctive that it will clash with other furnishings. In fact, one of the key benefits of this particular table is that it blends so easily with most interior design styles. Whether you've put together a mid-century modern home or have opted for a more conventional traditional style, the table will look like a well-chosen member of your furniture ensemble.

The profile taper of the legs adds just the right amount of flair, and you can inject a personalized look by painting the table (complementary or contrasting colors in the top and base is an especially eye-catching look). But in most cases, finishing the table natural will be the more appealing look that works with the widest range of home styles.

WHAT YOU'LL NEED

Time: **30 minutes** | Difficulty: **Medium**

TOOLS:

Circular saw

Pocket hole jig

Measuring tape

Speed square

Carpenter's pencil

Metal straightedge

Power drill and bits

Hammer

Palm sander

Paintbrush (optional)

MATERIALS:

1 pallet

2 ½" pocket hole screws

Finish nails

100-grit sandpaper

Paint or stain (optional)

2. Measure 3" down from one end of a leg and use a speed square to mark a line at this point. Measure in 1¾" from an edge, along the opposite end of the leg, and mark this point at the end. (Adjust the length and angle of the taper as necessary to remove any notches or leave a portion of a notch as an interesting variation to a straight taper.) Repeat the process with all of the legs.

3. Use a straightedge to mark a line from the end mark to where the opposite mark intersects the edge of the leg. Repeat with the remaining legs, and cut them with a circular saw.

4. Cut four top boards 16" long from deck boards.

5. Construct the frame by screwing each short brace between the edges of two legs, with 2½" pocket hole screws. Connect the two leg pairs with long braces screwed to the inner faces of the legs. In both cases, the braces should be flush with the outside surfaces and tops of the legs.

6. Dry fit the top boards so that the overhang is exactly 1" all the way around. Mark the boards and the leg frame to key the positions of the top boards.

7. Starting from one side, lay a top board in position, key it to the marks, and drill pilot holes down into the braces and legs. Use finish nails to fasten the board to the leg frame. Repeat the process with the remaining boards.

8. Thoroughly sand the table all over, slightly rounding the ends and outside edges of the top boards. Prime and paint as desired, or finish with a stain or other product.

HOW YOU MAKE IT

1. Cut four legs 20" long from stringers. Cut two braces 7" long and two braces 11" long from a stringer. Use a pocket hole jig to drill two pocket holes at either end of each brace.

   Optional: If you have a planer or jointer, or a friend with that machinery, the final table will look much better and more polished if you plane and smooth the lumber before constructing the side table.

QUICK 3

It's easy to overlook the fact that deconstructed pallet wood can, when cleaned up, be quite handsome in its own right. Break a pallet down into its parts, and those parts can actually be decorative if used in the right way. Small home accents made with pallet wood can be lovely, especially when you put your own signature on them. These three projects are perfect examples. Not only are these creations interesting additions to any home (and incredibly useful, in the case of the cutting board), but they also make unique and touching gifts. Of course, they can also serve as departure points for your own creativity. Build on these ideas to use up scraps or odd-sized pieces leftover from other pallet projects, and you'll be upcycling like a true pro. No matter how you adapt the projects, you're going to discover making accents like these takes an amazingly small amount of time and effort.

1. TEA LIGHT CANDLEHOLDERS

Pallet-wood creations don't need to be big to be impressive. These tea light candleholders are proof positive of that. Small and charming, they are simply sections of a stringer, cut at angles to make small "boat" shapes. A two-inch spade bit is used to drill a three-quarters-inch deep hole right in the center of each shape, in which a tea light candle can sit. Play with the shape as you like—square it off for a blocky appeal, or use a jigsaw to create a sexier, more curved profile. If you want a more substantial decorative feature, leave a stringer whole and round off the corners and edges with a palm sander. Then use the spade bit to make tea light cavities spaced evenly along the length of the stringer. No matter what type of candleholders you craft, you can finish them in a

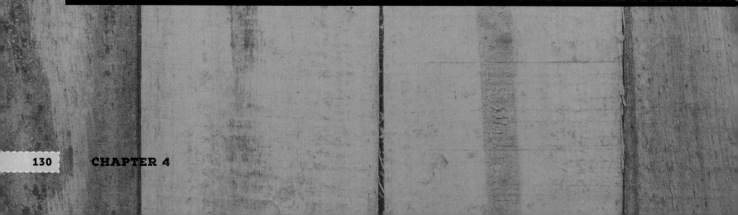

stain or natural finish, or go fun and fascinating with colored paints! Among the projects here, these are some of the most welcome gifts for birthdays, Christmas, and especially housewarming parties.

2. CUTTING BOARD

A cutting board is an essential addition to any kitchen. Although making one doesn't require much skill, it will require patience, some heavy-duty equipment and attention to detail. Decide on the width, length, and height of the cutting board first. Select a mix of stringer and deck boards that when cut will accommodate the board's dimensions. Then use a jointer to surface all the wood on four sides, making the pieces perfectly square. Cut and rip the pieces and align the final stock side to side to check the layout that will create the cutting board's pattern. When you're happy with the arrangement, face-glue the pieces together, clamping them until they're dry. Once dry, cut to final length, sand all around (making sure any glue squeeze-out is removed), and finish with multiple coats of tung oil, linseed oil, or other food-safe finish. You can use a food-safe stain to make alternating light and dark strips, or change the dimensions to create a longer

cutting board for larger surfaces or busier kitchens. You can even cut one end of the board with a jigsaw to form a handle. Drill a hole through the handle to hang the cutting board when not in use.

3. SERVING TRAY

A breakfast-in-bed serving tray is one of life's little luxuries that can easily provide an everyday function, bringing snacks and drinks to the TV-watching couch. The base is made from three deck boards cut twenty inches long (or however long you want). Rip deck boards in half and cut two 1 ¾" pieces to twenty inches and two fourteen inches long. Create a box frame by nailing the longer pieces overlapping the ends of the shorter pieces (drill pilot holes first) with finish nails. However, if the deck boards you're reclaiming are thinner than three-quarters inch, you may need to join the corners with steel L brackets. Then nail the four boards to the frame. Again, if the deck boards are too thin, modify the design with cleats around the top of the tray's bottom, ripped down from stringer scraps. The frame can then be nailed to the cleats. Add decorative handles on either end of the tray and you're set for brunch!

DOORMAT OR BATHMAT

A doormat is such a simple thing, but made well and put in the right place, you'll be grateful for it every day. This particular mat can also be used as a bathmat. It will fit particularly well with other real-wood accents, such as a tissue holder, shelves, or towel bars. But because of its height and the unforgiving nature of the wood it's made from, most people prefer to use it for a front- or back-entry door.

No matter where you use it, it is undeniably handsome. The mat is assembled with hidden fasteners, which means you'll have to get familiar with using a pocket hole jig. These are inexpensive tools and incredibly useful if you plan on making any furniture—or structures such as finely detailed fencing—in the future.

The measurements on such a small project are critical. Double-check all your measurements, and don't cut until you're sure you have it right. Be precise and you'll wind up with a bathmat or doormat that looks much better than anything you can buy at a store.

WHAT YOU'LL NEED

Time: **20 minutes** | Difficulty: **Easy**

TOOLS:

Table saw

Pocket hole jig

Speed square

Power drill and bits

Bar clamp

Measuring tape

Carpenter's pencil

Palm sander or sanding block

Paintbrush or soft cloth

Putty knife

MATERIALS:

1 pallet

Wood glue

1 ½" pocket hole screws

2 ½" pocket hole screws

Tung oil or other sealant, or sealing finish

Sandpaper

HOW YOU MAKE IT

1. Cut four frame pieces from deck boards: Two ends 16" long, and two sides 25" long. Rip the pieces down to 3" wide by removing about ¼" on each side to clean up the boards and square them off.

2. Cut five slats 10" long from deck boards. Rip them down to 3" wide in the same way you did the frame pieces.

3. Use a pocket hole jig to drill pocket holes in the frame end pieces and the ends of the slats.

4. Mark and miter the ends of the frame pieces 45° using a speed square. Coat the cut edges with wood glue, clamp the frame together upside down, and use 1½" pocket hole screws to fasten the frame pieces tightly together.

5. Place the frame upside down on a perfectly flat, level surface. Starting at ¹¹/₁₆" in from one end, measure and mark every 3 ¹¹/₁₆" along the length of both long frame pieces.

6. Set the slats in place between the frame sides. Align the slats with the marks on the frame edges, flush with the top of the frame. If any slats don't fit, sand both ends until they do. Screw them to the frame sides with 2½" pocket hole screws.

7. Scrape off any glue squeeze-out at the corners using a putty knife and sand the mat well, sloping the frame pieces slightly down toward the outside edges and rounding the corners. Seal the mat with tung oil, waterproofing, or similar finish.

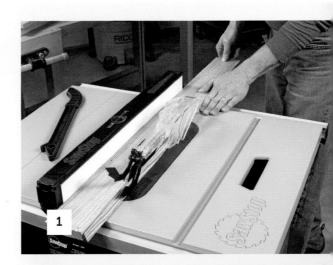

CLOCK

This "timely" creation can be customized in ways limited only by your imagination and is incredibly simple to construct. Really, though, this project is as much about pure fun as it is about getting your hands dirty making something for the house.

Clocks serve both a decorative and functional purpose. That's why it's the rare room in the house that doesn't benefit from a wall-hung clock. Creating one like the clock in this project is an opportunity to design a fantastic accent piece that stands out as strongly as art would on the wall. A clock such as this also makes a wonderful housewarming gift.

Consider the basics of this project as a launching ground for your own aesthetic. Paint the clock face in vivid colors, choose a distinctive font to stencil for the numbers, or play around with the look of the clock to suit your own décor. Just keep in mind that you can go wild with a design accent this small because it should pop out, not blend into, the rest of the room.

The widespread availability of clock kits that include a battery-motor casing and two hands makes constructing the clock easy. The actual assembly process shown here won't challenge your DIY skills and certainly won't take more than part of a Saturday afternoon.

WHAT YOU'LL NEED

Time: **20 minutes** | Difficulty: **Easy**

TOOLS:

Table saw or circular saw

2 bar clamps

Palm sander

Measuring tape

Carpenter's pencil

Paintbrush (optional)

Woodworking compass

Power drill and bits

Jigsaw

MATERIALS:

1 pallet

Clock kit with motor and

hands

Wood glue

100-grit sandpaper

1 ½" wood screws

Sawtooth frame hanger or similar

HOW YOU MAKE IT

1. Cut four 16"-long boards from deck boards; they must be free of serious flaws in the faces or edges. Check the post of the clock mechanism to ensure you can accommodate the thickness of your deck boards.

(You can rip down boards as necessary and adjust the measurements to accommodate by adding boards or decreasing the finished size of the clock—it's 14" here).

2. Edge glue the four boards together to create a 16" square. Clamp them with bar clamps

until they're dry. When dry, scrape or sand off any glue squeeze-out. Sand the boards smooth for the appearance you're after (leave them rougher for a more rustic look).

3. Measure 7" down from one end, along the center joint between the inner two boards. Mark this point and wedge a brad or small nail in the joint at the mark. Use a woodworking compass to draw a 14" diameter circle on the face of the boards. Repeat the process on the opposite side of the boards.

4. Use a jigsaw to cut out the clock shape, following the marked circle on the front of the boards. Paint or finish the face of the clock as desired.

5. Rip and cut a scrap of deck board into two 9" x 1¾" cleats. Measure 2¼" down from the top of the clock circle drawn on the back of the boards and draw a horizontal reference line. Do the same from the bottom of the circle.

6. Align the cleats flush to the reference lines and centered across the circle. Screw each cleat to the clock boards, using one 1½" wood screw per board.

7. Drill a clock motor post hole where you secured the nail for the compass (the kit shown here requires a ¼" hole; size the hole according to the post for the kit you're using). Test fit the motor and the hands, then stencil or mark numbers on the clock face to correspond with the hand positions.

8. Nail a sawtooth hanger or other hanger onto the back of the top cleat and hang the clock.

FLOATING SHELF

The popular, sleek look of this shelf seems to defy gravity. It juts out from the wall with no visible means of support—thus the name. In reality, the shelf relies on a strong hidden support structure, which in this case is composed of two-by-four stringers. That means that no matter what you put on the shelf, you'll never have to worry about it failing.

Although many floating shelves on the market are modest in size, this one has been designed with substantial dimensions. It could easily hold a row of coffee table books or a shelf stereo. (If you're going to use it for books, consider drilling holes for short dowels that will act as bookends to keep your library on the shelf.) In fact, the shelf would be excellent as a support for a flat-screen TV—a natural marriage because you can position the shelf for the optimal viewing height. You could even build several of these to hold not only the TV, but other related components.

No matter what you put on it, the look is cool. Although this one is stained, you could paint it the color of the wall to embellish the illusion of a floating surface organically projecting out from the vertical wall surface.

WHAT YOU'LL NEED

Time: **45 minutes** | Difficulty: **Medium**

TOOLS:

Table saw

Power drill and bits

Hammer

Speed square

Putty knife

Palm sander

Paintbrush

Measuring tape

Carpenter's pencil

Torpedo level

MATERIALS:

1 pallet

3" wood screws

C-clamps and bar clamps

Finish nails

Wood putty

100-grit sandpaper

Paint, stain, or other finish

HOW YOU MAKE IT

1. Rip a stringer down to 2" wide. Cut two arms 11¼" long and one brace 21" long from the stringer. Screw the arms to the ends of the bracket with 3" wood screws to form a *U*.

2. Cut seven shelf boards 25½" long and two 10½" long from deck boards. Mark and miter each end of six of the long boards 45° using the speed square. Rip a 45° bevel in the long edges of each short board.

3. Clamp three of the mitered long boards, tightly butted edge to edge, to a flat, level work surface. Hold the beveled edge of one short board perpendicular to the long boards, and drill at least two pilot holes per surface board along the side board's edge. Nail the side board to the surface boards with finish nails.

4. Repeat on the opposite ends of the surface boards, to fasten the second side board in place. Fasten the bottom surface boards in place to the side boards using the same process.

5. Drill pilot holes through the fascia board into the front edges of the shelf box, and nail the fascia board to the box.

6. Putty over the nail heads, let the putty dry, and sand the shelf box all over. Finish the box with a stain as shown here, paint, or other finish, as desired.

7. Locate the studs in the area of the wall where the shelf will be mounted. Measure and mark the location for the top of the shelf, and use a level to draw a reference line for the top.

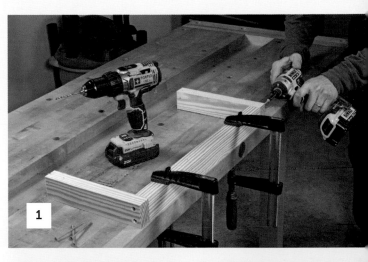

8. Align the shelf bracket with the line, check for level one last time, and screw the bracket to the studs with 3" wood screws.

9. Slip the shelf box over the bracket, and screw the box to the bracket along the wall mount side with 3" wood screws driven on the top and bottom back edge of the box. Dab paint or finish over the screw heads.

FLOATING SHELVES IN ROOM DESIGN

Floating shelves are a distinctively unique look. This style of shelving is streamlined and unobtrusive, and is the perfect solution in areas where actual bookcases would not fit or wouldn't be appropriate. Floating shelves are so innocuous that they are compatible with most interior design styles. But the truth is, they are ideally suited to some specific installations.

• **Inside corners.** The intersection of two walls can be lost space in a room. Bookcases are visually uncomfortable crammed into a corner, and seating is not practical. But floating shelves seem to dissolve into the meeting wall, allowing the most usable space of any solution and far more than any freestanding piece of furniture. The shelves also leave the corner visually open.

• **Nooks.** Small nooks or cutouts in a wall are perfect for floating shelves sized to fit. Nesting floating shelves inside a nook often creates the appearance of a built-in unit. It's also a wonderful way to turn an awkward space into incredibly useful storage. Because furniture rarely fits perfectly into a nook, you can often line the space with floor to ceiling floating shelves, creating a small library or a dedicated space for a figurine collection or other display pieces.

• **Kitchen.** There are a lot of advantages to using shelves in place of cabinets in a kitchen. Although conventional shelving units rarely find a comfortable home in the kitchen, floating shelves can be sized and placed exactly where you need them. They should be used to store lighter supplies and utensils—such as dry goods, paper products, or stemware—but the benefit is the same: you keep frequently used materials visible and right on hand so that they are easy to grab whenever you need them.

PET BOWL HOLDER

You have to love your big, shaggy best friends . . . until they start to polish off dinner. Let's face it, dogs just aren't neat eaters. From the moment that tail starts wagging to seconds after all the food has been inhaled, a dog eating is a festival of mess. Water may be splashed across your floor, and errant pieces of dried dog food find their way outside the bowl. (And some cats aren't much neater.)

The pet bowl holder in this project helps prevent the mess in two ways. First, it stops the bowls from moving and sloshing as they do. Second, it raises the food dishes closer to the level of the dog's snout, which makes for a less messy chow time.

Thanks to the sturdy nature of pallet wood, the holder can be used indoors or out. You can finish or paint the base, but leave the top natural because your pet will probably be licking the top. Of course, it's usually easier to leave the whole structure natural, especially if it will be normally kept out of sight in a mudroom, utility space, or pantry.

WHAT YOU'LL NEED

Time: **30 minutes** | Difficulty: **Medium**

TOOLS:		MATERIALS:
Table saw or circular saw	Woodworking compass	1 pallet
Router	Power drill and bits	Wood glue
Dado blade set	Jigsaw	3″ wood screws
Bar clamps	Sanding block	Sandpaper
Carpenter's pencil		Pet bowls

HOW YOU MAKE IT

1. Cut two frame sides 21″ long and two frame ends 9″ long from stringers. Cut three top boards 19″ long from deck boards.

2. Use a table saw equipped with a dado blade (or a router with a guide) to cut ¾″ wide by ¼″ deep dados in the faces of the frame pieces, 1″ in from an edge (along the edge opposite any notches).

3. Edge glue and clamp the top boards aligned side to side. When dry, mark points on the surface 5″ in from each end and centered side to side. Use a woodworking compass to scribe each bowl dircle, centered around the marks.

4. Drill a starter hole in each circle, and use a jigsaw to cut out the circles.

5. Butt a frame end to the end of a frame side to create one corner (with the dados aligned and the notches facing down), and fasten them together with 3" wood screws. Repeat with the opposite frame end piece to create a *U*.

6. Slide the glued top into the dado slot. Slide the remaining frame side onto the top, and screw it to the frame ends on both sides. Sand to remove obvious blemishes and splinters, but don't finish the frame, because your pet will be licking it, so you'll need to avoid possibly toxic coatings.

Resources

European Pallet Association (EPAL)
www.epal-pallets.org

National Wooden Pallet and Container Association
www.palletcentral.com
(703) 519-6104

Western Pallet Association
www.westernpallet.org
(360) 335-0208

About the Author

Chris Peterson is a freelance writer and editor based in the Pacific Northwest. He has written extensively on home improvement and general reference topics, including books in the Black & Decker Complete Guide series; *Building with Secondhand Stuff: How to Re-Claim, Re-Vamp, Re-Purpose & Re-Use Salvaged & Leftover Building Materials*; *Practical Projects for Self-Sufficiency: DIY Projects to Get Your Self-Reliant Lifestyle Started*; and *Manskills: How to Avoid Embarrassing Yourself and Impress Everyone Else*. When he's not writing or editing, Chris spends his time hiking, baking, and rooting for the New York Yankees.

Index

Page numbers in *italics* refer to figures.